The Myth of *Silent Spring*

The publisher and the University of California Press Foundation gratefully acknowledge the generous support of the Ralph and Shirley Shapiro Endowment Fund in Environmental Studies.

The Myth of *Silent Spring*

Rethinking the Origins of American Environmentalism

Chad Montrie

UNIVERSITY OF CALIFORNIA PRESS

University of California Press, one of the most distinguished university presses in the United States, enriches
lives around the world by advancing scholarship in the
humanities, social sciences, and natural sciences. Its
activities are supported by the UC Press Foundation and
by philanthropic contributions from individuals and
institutions. For more information, visit www.ucpress.edu.

University of California Press
Oakland, California

Library of Congress Cataloging-in-Publication Data

Names: Montrie, Chad, author.
Title: The myth of Silent Spring : rethinking the origins
    of American environmentalism / Chad Montrie.
Description: Oakland, California : University of
    California Press, [2018] | Includes bibliographical
    references and index.
Identifiers: LCCN 2017044530 (print) | LCCN 2017048585
    (ebook) | ISBN 9780520965157 (ebook) | ISBN
    9780520291331 (unjacketed cloth : alk. paper) |
    ISBN 9780520291348 (pbk. : alk. paper)
Subjects: LCSH: Environmentalism—United States—
    History.
Classification: LCC GE197 (ebook) | LCC GE197 .M66 2018
    (print) | DDC 363.700973—DC23
LC record available at https://lccn.loc.gov/2017044530

Manufactured in the United States of America

26 25 24 23 22 21 20 19 18
10 9 8 7 6 5 4 3 2 1

For Dale Billingsley

CONTENTS

ACKNOWLEDGMENTS

The Myth of "Silent Spring" would not have seen the light of day without the early and continuous enthusiastic support of Kate Marshall, an acquisition editor at the University of California Press. I am truly glad we decided to meet for coffee at the American Society for Environmental History conference back in 2015. Likewise, once I had a draft finished, editorial assistant Bradley Depew helped in all manner of ways to steer the manuscript through the UC board approval process. His advice and diligence were critical for getting the book to the last stage. Senior editor Kate Hoffman and editorial assistant Zuha Khan also proved to be exceptionally professional and competent in dealing with many other aspects of publication. And lastly, I could not have had a better copy editor than Anne Canright. She does incredibly attentive and careful work.

During the formal proposal stage for *The Myth of "Silent Spring,"* Kathryn Morse and David Stradling offered numerous astute observations through several different iterations, some of which led me to dramatically change what I thought I was going to do. Certainly, the book would have been a lesser one without their role in bringing it to print. Also, like almost all of the other things I have published in my academic career, *The Myth of "Silent Spring"* has its origins in ongoing conversations with my mentor and friend John Cumbler. He was one of the first historians to demonstrate the promise of blending "new" labor and social history with environmental history, and I have tried my best to follow his lead. Additionally, I want to thank another mentor and friend, Dale Billingsley. He has taught me a great deal about meaningful intellectual engagement, and that is why the book is dedicated to him.

Over the past two and a half decades, as I traveled a daunting course from being a college student to teaching at a university, my family has been a steady source of comfort and aid. My mother, stepfather, sisters, and of course my daughter Phoebe, each in their own particular way, make it possible for me to do the work I do. My partner (and emergency contact), Kristen Harol, is another person whom I count on every day. Although she will not be receiving any royalties, to her credit she's the one who kept telling me I had to write this particular book, and so I did. Finally, I want to posthumously thank Rachel Carson as well, for writing and defending *Silent Spring.* It took a lot of courage for her to brave the chauvinistic arrogance of male scientists as well as to challenge the blind greed of pesticide industry defenders. I realize that writing my own book required no such thing.

Introduction

*"The Fight for a Balanced Environment
and the Fight for Social Justice and Dignity
Are Not Unrelated Struggles"*

In the early part of 1962, Houghton Mifflin editor Paul Brooks asked U.S. Supreme Court justice William O. Douglas to write a review of Rachel Carson's manuscript for *Silent Spring*, a methodical indictment of synthetic pesticides. Among the lines Brooks picked from the review to compose a jacket endorsement, Douglas acclaimed the environmental exposé "the most revolutionary book since *Uncle Tom's Cabin*." Similarly, when *Silent Spring* was finally published, famed children's author and essayist E. B. White predicted that it would be "an *Uncle Tom's Cabin* of a book,—the sort that will help turn the tide." Both were referring to Harriet Beecher Stowe's startling portrait of slavery, written a century earlier, which many believed had prompted the white South to secede and take up arms against the North. On meeting Stowe at the White House, President Abraham Lincoln had supposedly greeted her by saying, "So this is the little lady who started this great war." Connecticut senator Abraham Ribicoff later alluded to that particular encounter when he opened a congressional subcommittee meeting about pesticides and other environmental hazards. "You are the lady who started all this," he said to Carson. "Will you please proceed?"[1]

Even before many people had actually read her book, it seems, eminent intellectuals, public officials, and various others were anointing the popular science writer as the single-most important galvanizing force behind an emergent environmental movement. Unfortunately, Rachel Carson did not get to live with *Silent Spring* and its impact for long. Midway through writing the final draft she was diagnosed with breast cancer, which metastasized to her lymph nodes, and two years after the book came out she died. In the interim, exhausting radiation treatments and debilitating infections made it increasingly difficult for her to travel and be publicly active. So when the National Wildlife Federation (NWF) held its annual conference in Detroit in March of 1963 and Carson canceled as a keynote speaker, the NWF had to find a replacement. Executive Director Thomas Kimball did not need to look far. He asked Detroit-based United Auto Workers (UAW) president Walter Reuther to fill in, and Reuther gladly agreed. At the conference, NWF president Dr. Paul A. Herbert gushingly introduced him to the audience, lauding the working-class firebrand for his uncommon efforts "to help the common man." Taking the podium, Reuther described the modern environmental catastrophe that humanity was facing, much as Carson might have done but characterizing it as a matter of social and economic justice. "There is a feeling of utmost urgency," he insisted, "in the war against selfishness, greed, and apathy in meeting the ever-increasing needs of the people," and he finished by pointing out the slow and inadequate efforts to control and abate industrial pollution.[2]

The next year, when President Lyndon Johnson delivered his "Great Society" speech at the University of Michigan's commencement ceremony, Reuther was invited to be on the stage, since the two men shared hopes of ending poverty in America and ridding the nation of racism. Shortly after, in the fall of 1965, the labor leader opened a UAW-sponsored "United Action for Clean Water Conference," an event attended by more than a thousand delegates representing a variety of labor unions, sportsmen's clubs, environmental organizations, and civic groups, the largest of its kind to date, and he invoked Johnson's resonant words. "A great society," Reuther declared, "is a society more concerned with the quality of its goals than the quantity of its goods." But, he lamented, the marketplace was becoming the only measure of good. To avert disaster there needed to be a "grand crusade," following a new set of values, with people mobilized at the community, state, and national levels to fight for clean water, pure air, and livable cities, challenging recalcitrant governments and irresponsible industry.[3] Subsequently, in 1967, Reuther had the UAW establish a Department of Conservation and Resource Development. The union did this, department director Olga Madar explained, "because our members and their families are directly affected by the environment around them, both inside and outside of the plants in which they work." Yet the UAW was not concerned exclusively with its own membership. "Air and water pollution, the desecration of our land, and the unwise use of our natural resources," Madar said, "are of great concern to us all."[4]

Just as Carson's voice was silenced by untimely death, however, Walter Reuther's own environmental advocacy was also cut short by unexpected tragedy. At the end of the 1960s, he had convinced the UAW executive board to replace the union's aging lake retreat at Port Huron, outside of Detroit, with a new labor education and vacation center at the more remote Black Lake. This would be "a thing of beauty," he hoped, "where man and nature can live in harmony." But only one week after he spoke to University of Michigan students on the first Earth Day, in April 1970, Reuther flew with his wife, an architect, and a few others to see the nearly finished building, and their plane crashed as it was landing, killing everyone on board. Nevertheless, the UAW went ahead with a planned environmental meeting at Black Lake that same year, in July, cosponsored by Environmental Action, the national group that had coordinated the Earth Day happenings. The weekend prior, the UAW and various conservation and environmental groups had delivered a nineteen-point plan to every U.S. senator, including a call for regulating industrial and auto emissions and improving mass transportation. At the conference—attended by students, community activists, and labor leaders—workshops focused primarily on "urban and industrial pollution" as well as the educational, legal, and political methods to force reforms. Victor Reuther, Walter's brother, closed the meeting and received a standing ovation when he called on "working people and students" to join together against the "cold and calculated" strategy of industry and their allies to divide them.[5]

Throughout the next decade, Conservation Department director Olga Madar oversaw continued efforts to enact more environmental legislation as well as encourage labor unions, environmental organizations, and consumer groups to develop a common agenda. She had some initial success in 1971, when Michigan senator Philip Hart organized the Urban Environment Conference (UEC), which included the United Auto Workers, United Steel Workers, and Oil, Chemical, and Atomic Workers, as well as the Sierra Club and National Welfare Rights Organization. Several years later, some of those participants helped form Environmentalists for Full Employment (EFFE), and in the spring of 1976 the UAW, UEC, and EFFE hosted another meeting at Black Lake, which they titled "Working for Environmental and Economic Justice and Jobs." This was not as well attended as the 1970 conference, and discordant comments from some participants suggested that the weakening economy and other factors were starting to take their toll on inclusive environmentalism. Yet the very fact of the gathering, and per-haps the presence of people like Friends of the Earth leader David Brower, demonstrated the open movement's hardiness. Greeting the few hundred activists assembled, the new UAW president, Leonard Woodcock, echoed his predecessor, claim-ing "common cause between union members and environmen-talists—between workers, poor people, minorities, and those seeking to protect our natural resources."[6]

"A REVOLUTIONARY BOOK"

As the brief chronicle of events above shows, United Auto Work-ers president Walter Reuther played a critical role in making and shaping the American environmental movement, and over the course of more than a decade he and Olga Madar worked dili-gently to keep the UAW at its center. What's more, their efforts were not unknown at the time. They were recognized by preser-vation and conservation groups, applauded by other union lead-ers and members, welcomed by sympathetic public officials in state legislatures, Congress, regulatory agencies, and the White House, and regularly profiled in print and broadcast media. So how we tend to remember the origins of environmentalism today is perplexing. Rarely if ever do we pay attention to the particular ways in which working people experienced environmental problems, and equally rarely do we acknowledge the efforts workers, their unions, and labor leaders made to address those problems, beginning at least as early as the 1940s. The standard interpretation of the American environmental movement's origins has changed little since *Silent Spring*'s publication in 1962, unfailingly repeating the claims that the book—as well as a CBS television documentary "The Silent Spring of Rachel Carson," broadcast in April 1963—"turned the tide" and "started it all."

Among academics there is a near consensus about *Silent Spring* and its historical significance. Carson's biographer brands it "a revolutionary book" and credits it with seeding "a powerful social movement that would alter the course of American history."[7] A second, well-respected historian claims, "No single event played a greater role in the birth of modern environmentalism than the publication of Rachel Carson's *Silent Spring* and its assault on insecticides."[8] Another scholar calls the book "one of the most politically and culturally influential in American history" and commends Carson "for being the godmother of the Environmental Protection Agency, the ban on DDT and other pesticides, Earth Day, the 1972 Federal Insecticide, Fungicide, and Rodenticide Act, and indeed of 'Environmentalism' as a philosophy and political movement."[9] A fourth cites "Rachel Carson's eloquent book" for dramatizing "the elemental interdependence of life on the planet," revealing the ecological underpinnings of "modern consumer society," and laying the groundwork for the environmental movement.[10] And one historian boldly insists that the book launched the "modern global environmental movement," inspiring and widening activism in the United States and "creating an environmental awareness" around the world.[11]

This "big book" origin story is ubiquitous beyond academic circles as well. To mark *Silent Spring*'s fiftieth anniversary, in 2012, for example, the *New York Times Magazine* ran a story titled "How 'Silent Spring' Ignited the Environmental Movement," claiming that the book's celebrated author "influenced the environmental movement as no one had since the 19th century's most celebrated hermit, Henry David Thoreau, wrote about Walden Pond."[12] Across the Atlantic that same year, the *Guardian* hailed *Silent Spring* as "one of the most effective denunciations of industrial malpractice ever written" and acknowledged that it is "widely credited with triggering popular ecological awareness in the US and Europe." The story quotes former Friends of the Earth director Jonathon Porritt heralding Carson as the first person to give voice to the notion that human beings had acquired the power to damage the natural world, as well as novelist (and social activist) Doris Lessing saying that the American scientist "was the originator of ecological concerns."[13]

Children's literature is also suffused with the standard dogma, obvious by titles alone, including *Rachel Carson: Pioneer of Ecology, Rachel Carson: Founder of the Environmental Movement,* and *Rachel Carson and Her Book That Changed the World.* The last, published in 2013, ends with a dense, small-print "Epilogue," apparently for adults, explaining that *Silent Spring* "opened the minds of millions to what was considered to be a new concept at the time: what we do to the air, water, and soil directly affects us, future generations, and animals and plants that share the earth with us."[14] Another book, aimed at early elementary readers, has the unassuming title *Rachel: The Story of Rachel Carson,* but it finishes with the customary sweeping claim. "It is generally agreed," the author confidently states, "that today's environmental movement began with the publication of *Silent Spring.*"[15]

Most if not all of the scholarly and popular accounts frame Carson's efforts to enlighten the American public as both extraordinarily prescient and heroically solitary. By their lights, her personal love of nature and training as a marine biologist gave

Carson an ecological consciousness that was very much contrary to prevailing assumptions of the day. And well-honed writing skills allowed her to single-handedly convince millions to adopt this sensibility, despite the arrogant vocal opposition of male scientists and a carefully crafted misinformation campaign waged by a powerful pesticide industry. Even existing conservation groups (the National Wildlife Federation among them) supposedly failed to come to Carson's defense.[16] To many residents of postwar suburbs, however, *Silent Spring* was a "shocking revelation," one that galvanized them to join and remake old conservation organizations (like the NWF and Sierra Club) and to establish new environmental groups (like the Environmental Defense Fund and Friends of the Earth). This growing awareness and activist inclination became more apparent as the 1960s drew to a close, culminating with the first Earth Day, the moment that truly transformed what was still purportedly "inchoate" and "fragmented" engagement into a national movement that subsequently became the main dynamic force supporting a whole range of new federal environmental laws.[17]

To be sure, Rachel Carson did contribute to making American environmentalism. She introduced some readers (and viewers) to the concept that all living things are connected to one another and their physical environment, a scientific principle not original to her but one she articulated with clarity and authority. Her particular case centered on the countless ill effects of pesticides, yet in outlining that she demonstrated its wider cogency. More concretely, *Silent Spring* prompted President Kennedy to establish an advisory committee, which issued a report, "The Use of Pesticides," in May 1963, pointing out certain benefits of pesticides but supporting the claim that much was unknown about their potentially harmful effects. Around the same time, several congressional committees organized hearings and proposed legislation, some of which passed, including a bill requiring consultation between the U.S. Fish and Wildlife Service and state wildlife agencies before spraying, another establishing guidelines for better labeling and ensuring closer evaluation of chemicals used as pesticides, and one that prevented manufacturers from marketing pesticides without U.S. Department of Agriculture (USDA) registration. Later, in 1972, the newly formed Environmental Protection Agency banned most domestic application of DDT, and in 1976 the Toxic Substances Control Act established more comprehensive regulation for a range of chemical products.[18]

While it is reasonable to credit Rachel Carson with helping to popularize ecology as well as influence environmental regulatory policy, however, it stretches facts to claim that she brought the American environmental movement into being. Putting her at the center of the story, or putting *Silent Spring* there, substitutes a simple yet appealing mythology for a more complicated account of what actually happened. The conventional version of events not only exaggerates Carson and her book's historical importance (a mostly harmless error) but also fundamentally misunderstands environmentalism's full history (a greater error with real present-day implications). It does not properly explain the movement's origins (the "why") or correctly date it (the "when") or fully consider the wide range of historical actors involved (the "who"). That is, it misses the mark for the main questions that historians struggle to answer when crafting any sound interpretation of change over time, one faithful to the available historical evidence and carefully constructed according to certain standards of scholarship.

In the *Silent Spring* origin story the emphasis is on how unintended consequences of post–World War II technological advances made the environmental movement necessary. Nuclear tests (part of a Cold War weapons race) filled the atmosphere with radioactive fallout, automobiles demanded ever-expanding road networks and produced noxious exhaust, other consumer goods (often plastic) added to the waste stream, tract housing construction (sustained by postwar federal mortgage guarantees) threatened to transform millions of acres of wetlands, hillsides, and floodplains, and pesticides (which had their origins in chemical warfare research) brought toxins directly to people's bucolic neighborhoods, yards, and homes. The standard narrative also highlights suburbanization—the move to the bucolic places—as the primary experience galvanizing consciousness and protest. During the 1950s and 1960s, white, middle-class Americans migrated from city to suburb by the millions, carrying a supposedly new regard for "quality of home and leisure," and the contrast between those values and the new looming threats to the natural environment and human well-being was stark. It was this contrast that Carson so adeptly presented in an attempt to effect change, calling on readers to save songbirds and themselves from an imminent chemical-laden apocalypse, and they eagerly responded by making an environmental movement.[19]

By exclusively concentrating on the postwar era, though, the familiar telling overlooks America's longer environmental transformation by industrialization. From its beginning in the nineteenth century, industrial manufacturing consumed vast amounts of natural resources and generated considerable amounts of noxious waste. Textile and paper mills, iron foundries, leather tanneries, cartridge (i.e., munition) factories, slaughterhouses, and other industry dumped millions of gallons of wastewater—laden with scouring chemicals, spent dyes, curing liquors, lubricant oil, and animal parts—directly into local streams and rivers.

There it mixed with raw sewage and household refuse from the thousands of workers drawn to bustling cities for jobs, living (and dying) in dense quarters with only primitive municipal sanitation services. This turned the waterways into "sewer basins," often the source of drinking water for downstream communities, and that made them a highly effective means to communicate water-born pathogens. As a result, the ever-increasing and ever-growing industrial towns and cities saw recurrent deadly disease epidemics (like cholera and typhoid), besides elevated rates of illness and death from other "crowd" diseases (such as tuberculosis and diphtheria).

Worsening conditions eventually generated widespread apprehension and state intervention. In New England in the years after the Civil War, public health crusaders organized city and state boards of health and pushed for pollution control laws. Henry Ingersoll Bowditch, a self-proclaimed "radical" who chaired the Massachusetts board, pitched these efforts as a logical expansion of traditional American rights. "We believe that all citizens have an inherent right to the enjoyment of pure and uncontaminated air, and water, and soil," he explained, "and that no one should be allowed to trespass upon it by his carelessness, or his avarice, or even his ignorance." Persuaded by that appeal, in 1878 the Massachusetts legislature passed a law prohibiting the discharge of untreated industrial waste and sewage into the state's streams and rivers. Not surprisingly, manufacturers saw the legislation as a threat, and they convinced the governor to merge the board of health with the boards of lunacy and charity and appoint a corporate lawyer as the new board's chair. Less than a decade later, however, lawmakers reestablished a separate board of health and enacted a measure expanding health officials' authority to oversee water quality for all inland waters, again affirming the principle of state regulatory action to address environmental problems.[20]

By the turn of the next century, much of the focus on water pollution in Massachusetts had shifted to purifying drinking water. Ellen Swallow Richards—the first woman to enroll at the Massachusetts Institute of Technology, the first woman to teach there, and a founder of both "sanitary" chemistry and bacteriology— played a critical role in this area. She oversaw the work of a group of scientists at a newly organized experiment station perched on the banks of the Merrimack River in Lawrence. There they conducted tests of various filtering methods, aeration techniques, and coagulation agents, many of them quite successful. Subsequently, in 1907 the city began cleaning all of its daily water supply, significantly lowering mortality from water-borne disease and prompting other cities across the country to follow their lead. Most hesitated to treat their raw sewage, though, since there was no advantage in it for them, and mills and factories continued to dump manufacturing wastes into rivers and streams without restraint. These pollution problems lingered until later, in New England and elsewhere, although when state and federal governments did begin to address them in the 1930s, throughout the region and across the United States, there was already well-established precedent for public responsibility and regulatory law.

In fact, accounts of environmentalism that venerate *Silent Spring* as a pivotal centerpiece not only miss the growing environmental awareness prompted by industrialization but also exhibit a striking disregard for the earlier activism that it provoked, even neglecting what was happening on the very eve of the book's publication. In a speech at the National Parks Association's annual meeting, Carson herself acknowledged how her interest in the dangers of pesticides came partly from letters people had sent to her pleading that she do something about federal spraying programs in their neighborhoods. And in her book and other public appearances she alluded to the importance of a 1957 lawsuit by some Long Island residents to stop the USDA from spraying in their community.[21] Yet neither *Silent Spring* itself, nor the public conversation about the book or the histories of environmentalism that feature it, gives any real sense of the many citizen campaigns that were already working on a whole range of environmental problems. If *Silent Spring* had an impact, however, it was because it appeared in a receptive place and time, in the same way that Harriet Beecher Stowe's *Uncle Tom's Cabin* contributed to a long-established abolitionist movement. Certainly by the mid-twentieth century a considerable portion of the American public had realized that modern industrial "progress" needed to be calibrated and controlled to protect humankind and the rest of the natural world, and countless numbers of people had started to do something about it, without Carson's prompting, inspiration, or guidance.

In the southern Appalachian coalfields, for example, during the 1940s and 1950s local residents were waging an increasingly militant fight against new surface mining methods, one way industrialization had come to the countryside. Early on in eastern Ohio, farmers and their rural allies joined together to challenge operators who leased land, scoured the topsoil for the coal below, and left without doing proper reclamation (or sometimes without doing any at all). Wellsville legislator William F. Daugherty first proposed a control bill to deal with this in 1937, and others followed, but it was not until after World War II that support was strong enough to actually get a law passed. "The demand for legislation to regulate coal stripping has come from the people," the editor for the *Cadiz Republican* declared, and their campaign was "a cry for self-preservation." As one local farm woman explained, what once was a pastoral countryside was fast being ruined. The lovely fields had been turned upside down, she said, "farm homes destroyed and in their places [were] those awful unsightly piles of dirt." As Ohio State Grange Master Joseph Fichter and many others pointed out, this "exploitation of people and our God-given natural resources" was particularly short-sighted, sacrificing otherwise plentiful natural resources as well as the health of entire communities for a quick profit. Governor Frank Lausche agreed (he once described stripping as "sheer butchery, disemboweling the land and leaving its ugly entrails exhibited to the naked eye"), and he very willingly signed the control bill the legislature passed in 1947.[22]

Similarly, in western Pennsylvania, where an adolescent Rachel Carson once roamed the hills to go bird watching, conservation-minded sportsmen got a control law passed in 1945. A decade and a half later, and a full year before the publication of *Silent Spring,* deep miners and other workers, many of them hunters and anglers themselves, joined together to enact even stricter regulatory legislation in the face of considerable coal operator resistance. "We are unequivocally opposed," the Allegheny County Labor Committee declared at one point, "to the selfish interests and to the legislators they appear to control who resist effective regulation of strip mining, [which] despoils our natural resources and endangers the health and lives of our citizens." The deep miners were watching their jobs disappear to the more efficient, nonunion, unregulated strip mines, which also ravaged local communities with deforestation, landslides, acid runoff, and other environmental effects. Worried that lobbying alone would not be enough to get a law passed, someone (possibly a miner or group of miners familiar with explosives) resorted to industrial sabotage. One night in July 1961 they dynamited a power shovel and bulldozer at a Fayette County strip mine. Shortly after, Senator John Haluska, a friend of one of the state's largest surface mine operators, received a death threat for holding a proposed regulatory bill in his committee. The note warned him to stop dithering and set an August 8 deadline, and it was signed "an honest sportsman who is a good shot with a gun." Haluska took this threat seriously and released the bill with just two days to spare. Then, when it got held up in the assembly, United Mine Workers District 5 president Jock Yablonski and other union officials intervened, putting pressure on the holdouts, and legislators finally passed the improved law.[23]

Of course, by excluding activism like the campaign against strip mining in Appalachia from the history of environmentalism, we not only get the cause and timing of the movement wrong but also fail to see the full set of historical actors who made it. The "big book" interpretation assumes a "great man" (or rather, a "great woman") understanding of historical change. It privileges the writings of a lone scientist, missing the many other countless ordinary people who contemplated, worried over, and acted to address various environmental problems. Without question, some individuals did have an outsized role in seeding and growing American environmentalism—from Henry Ingersoll Bowditch and Ellen Swallow Richards in the nineteenth century to Walter Reuther and Olga Madar in the twentieth, as well as Rachel Carson—and they should be prominently included in any historical record. Fixing on one person, or just a handful, however, cannot truly explain change or continuity over time. History is usually made by a dynamic interplay between a select few acting "from the top down" and a mass of people acting "from the bottom up," and often the efforts from below are more important, especially when it comes to social movements. That was certainly true for environmentalism, which took root and spread largely because of common people's efforts. This was not because they read a particular book or heard a certain speech or watched a television program but (initially, at least) because they were driven by their own actual circumstances. And sometimes they thought and acted contrary to those who were most famously recognized for defining an environmental ethic and leading environmental organizations.

In southern California, for instance, where decades of land consolidation and the adoption of industrial farming methods had effectively created "factories in the field," migrant Mexican and Mexican American farmworkers joined together in a union campaign that lasted throughout the 1960s and into the 1970s and intentionally attempted to attract environmental allies. The workers' primary grievances were meager wages, long hours, and inadequate housing as well as makeshift or nonexistent protection from exposure to pesticides and herbicides. Since the campaign coincided with the rise of the *chicano* empowerment movement, they also linked their health concerns to a pattern of racial discrimination, an important connection that other activists would later term "environmental racism."

The California Department of Public Health (CDPH) first investigated agricultural chemical poisoning in 1949, when two dozen pear pickers were sickened by exposure to parathion. Even without correcting for the high rate of underreporting, within a decade agriculture had the highest rate of occupational disease among all the state's industries, most of that concentrated in the counties with the largest number of migrant farmworkers. Oddly, though, with the exception of a few brief lines, Rachel Carson paid little attention to the plight of these or any other workers in *Silent Spring.* What's more, the lobbying she did, along with the government response it prompted, led growers to switch from chemicals that, though less persistent, were more acutely toxic when applied, providing greater protection for consumers while increasing the risks to field hands (and other living things nearby). By the mid-1960s, when the CDPH did another survey, 71 percent of farmworkers questioned had some symptom of chemical-related illness, from itching and chills to headaches and stomach pains.[24]

As conditions in the fields and orchards became increasingly intolerable, community activists César Chávez and Dolores Huerta came to the San Joaquin Valley and founded the National Farm Workers Association, eventually combining forces with the primarily Filipino Agricultural Workers Organizing Committee to form the United Farm Workers Organizing Committee. Together, they helped thousands of field hands march, picket, and strike for union recognition and collective bargaining rights, but it was a difficult struggle. Growers, public officials, and police colluded to intimidate, beat, and jail activists, and so the workers solicited outside support. Early on, Walter Reuther made a visit with a check from the UAW for $10,000 as well as a pledge to contribute $5,000 a month, and later his union bankrolled a short film, *Brothers and Sisters,* which farmworker organizers used to tour the country. Meanwhile, volunteer nurse Marion Moses established a health and safety commission to investigate pesticide exposure, and California Rural Legal Assistance lawyer Ralph Abascal examined spray application records, lab analyses, and lawsuits, assembling a critical mass of evidence. Drawing on that work, in 1965 the newly renamed United Farm Workers (UFW) called for a consumer boycott of table grapes, with a stunning pamphlet titled "The Poisons We Eat."[25]

Notwithstanding seemingly common interests, however, the UFW repeatedly encountered hesitation from "environmental" and "ecology" activists. When a radical Berkeley group made an "Ecology Walk" against "agri-chemical powers" in 1970, organizers kept their distance from striking workers, to "maintain a safe neutrality" and "reach all the people they wanted to reach." Some of the marchers ignored the plan, split from the procession midway, and went to an Easter mass in Delano, where union members applauded their disobedience. "The farm workers' struggle," they insisted, "is a valid and important part of Ecology."[26] Mostly, though, attempts to explain the logic of solidarity fell on deaf ears, and local and national environmental groups continued to exhibit cautious reluctance in the decade following. "Surely," one frustrated UFW staff member wrote in a letter to the Environmental Defense Fund (EDF), "the fight for a balanced environment and the fight for social justice and dignity are not unrelated struggles."[27] Leaders at the EDF, Sierra Club, and other organizations claimed to agree, yet they did little or nothing to lend their membership and resources to the campaign.[28]

"A MATTER OF DEFINITION"

Just as United Farm Worker organizers were perplexed by environmental leaders' reluctance to broaden their perspective, it might seem puzzling why it has been so difficult to get historians, journalists, children's authors, and others to adopt a more inclusive interpretation of environmentalism's origins. The root of the problem in both cases is a matter of definition—who counts as an "environmentalist" and what counts as "environmentalism." Many of those who are part of the environmental movement or who are contributing to telling the movement's story simply cannot imagine that workers and the poor and people who are not white might have an environmental sensibility or that they might participate in environmental protest, whether past or present. They also have trouble regarding the typically multifold concerns of working people, the impoverished, African Americans, Latinos, and others as properly environmental, discounting any effort that explicitly links environmental problems and economic or social injustice, or labeling it as something else. Consequently, activists are challenged to expand environmentalism's ranks and enlarge its agenda, and historians are challenged to see anything other than the flawed version of the environmental movement's founding and unfolding, one focused mostly on the white middle-class and limited to their particular interests.

This narrow perspective is clear in the stark absence of African Americans from almost all accounts of wilderness preservation, resource conservation, and environmental activism. In part, the absence reflects their somewhat marginal place in each. Many past leaders, organizations, and followers associated with those endeavors were white, and they presumed that only white (elite) people had the civic-mindedness, appreciation of beauty, and concern for the future to care about the natural world. Oftentimes they matched this presumption with an explicit unwillingness to welcome black participation as well as active efforts to exclude blacks from their ranks. "The pot-hunting Negro," lamented game conservation advocate Charles Askins in 1909, "has all the skill of the Indian, has more industry in his loafing, and kills without pity and without restraint." They hunted for food, he explained, not for sport, and once guns became more readily available, they began to decimate local songbird populations, prompting southern sportsmen to complain, "The niggers are killing our quail."[29] Meanwhile, the Prairie Club, the Midwest equivalent to the Sierra Club in the West and Appalachian Trail Club in the East, stated that its wilderness activities were "open to white people of any nationality or creed."[30]

In the face of the color line's extension to these arenas of public life, some blacks simply created separate organizations, conjoining appreciation of nature with racial defiance. In 1923, for example, seventeen African American residents of St. Paul established the Gopher Gun Club, "to protect game fish and wild birds of all varieties" and to secure "adequate hunting grounds to meet the demand of the Northwest sportsman." Their hope was to purchase 600 acres outright to serve as a "hunting reserve and fishing point," and they planned to erect cottages there for members to bring their friends and families on weekend trips and longer vacations. If that proved too difficult, however, they intended to lease 1,000 acres from a local bank, which had already agreed to their terms. "The necessity of such a plan," the charter members declared, "should be obvious to every race person in the Twin Cities."[31]

In fact, the lack of African Americans in the narrative about environmentalism is also a failure to acknowledge black environmental thinking and protest that did happen, often because it somehow deviates from a standard "white" understanding of what warrants recognition. Environmental histories following in the footsteps of *Silent Spring* easily incorporate white suburban residents' objections to DDT spraying in their neighborhoods, for instance, but they tend not to include black activists' campaigns against lead poisoning caused by peeling paint in city slum apartments. Why? The latter very much resembles the former, except for race and place. In one of the very few historical accounts of the struggle to deal with lead, historian Robert

Gioielli details how activists in the northside ghettos of St. Louis worked diligently over the course of the 1960s and 1970s to set up blood tests for thousands of children and to push public officials to enact and enforce lead paint laws there. When they sought aid from scientist Barry Commoner at nearby Washington University, he helped them establish the Environmental Field Program, which hired African American Wilbur Thomas as the director. On the first Earth Day, in April 1970, Thomas gave a speech titled "Black Survival in our Polluted Cities," explaining the racist economic and political forces responsible for the environmental burden urban black Americans experienced. St. Louis passed its first lead law soon after, yet this proved too slow to adequately address the problem, since it split enforcement between the health department and housing division. Organizers then began a series of direct action protests led by the newly formed People's Coalition against Lead Poisoning, including sit-ins at realtors' offices and rent strikes against recalcitrant landlords. This eventually led to modifications in the law, Gioielli observes, although the changes still did not bring an end to lead poisoning, and the campaign continued at local, state, and national levels.[32]

The book you are reading now, *The Myth of "Silent Spring,"* is meant to provide a more accurate (but not comprehensive) history of the American environmental movement, incorporating stories like the black activists' lead campaign in St. Louis, Mexican and Mexican American farmworkers' pesticide battle in southern California, Appalachian mountain residents' struggle against surface coal mining, Michigan autoworkers' organizing against water pollution, and other critical yet slighted contributions to a tradition of environmental protest in this country. It is necessarily a "long" history, not by its actual length but rather by its scope, starting in the early nineteenth century, when industrialization began to create the environmental problems that spurred environmental awareness and galvanized environmental activism, and ending in our own century, when industrial capitalism is still the root cause of the most imminent and ominous environmental threats. This unusual recasting of environmentalism's past is essential because, at the very basic level, we should know what really happened, which is not what many think happened. The interpretation is more than an abstract or academic argument, however, since how we understand the environmental movement's history also guides how we conceptualize and do environmental activism in the present. Pushing the origins of environmental concerns back to the start of the modern industrial era, marking the ways class exploitation, racial inequality, and other forms of social injustice were inextricably linked to those evolving concerns, and acknowledging the role many ordinary people played in doing something about them—all of that enables us to better see the full complexity of environmental problems today and empowers us to shape our activism accordingly.[33]

The rest of the book following this introduction is organized into three chapters and a conclusion, arranged chronologically as well as topically, with an eye to helping readers easily follow the revisionist narrative they build. Each chapter begins with reference to an aspect of *Silent Spring,* to raise initial questions about environmentalism's traditional rendering and suggest how and why we need a different account. Chapter 1, "I Think Less of the Factory Than of My Native Dell," focuses on the environmental conflict that played out with the rise of industrial capitalism in New England during the nineteenth century and continues to follow that story in a few places out West. Chapter 2, "Why Don't

They Dump the Garbage on the Bully-Vards?," concentrates
mainly on the Midwest during the late nineteenth and early
twentieth centuries, as different groups of Americans continued
to develop their environmental thinking and organize themselves to confront various environmental problems. Chapter 3,
"Massive Mobilization for a Great Citizen Crusade," ranges
more widely by geography, sampling the vast array of environmental campaigns that occurred both before and after *Silent
Spring* was published. And the conclusion, "They Keep Threatening Us with the Loss of Our Jobs," highlights a particular way
that our stunted historical consciousness about environmentalism's origins and evolution hinders contemporary efforts to
organize an effective environmental movement, bringing history
to bear on the supposedly mutually exclusive choice of "jobs versus environment."

One thing that will become evident from chapter to chapter
is that the way people have thought about environmental problems, and what they have tried to do about them, varied from
place to place and changed over time. American environmentalism was certainly a polyglot and dynamic affair, containing a
whole host of ideas and approaches, manifested in wide-ranging
individual and group action. Talking about this as part of a single "environmental movement," however, does not inevitably
understate or overlook that diversity. Just as it is possible to better understand the rich variety of workers' consciousness and
organizing by considering it all as part of a "labor movement,"
framing environmentalism in a similar manner can actually
make its complexity more rather than less evident. It can also
draw attention to how different kinds of thinking about managing natural resource use, preserving wilderness, and controlling
pollution are interrelated, evolving from decade to decade,

building on one another, whether in hostile opposition or mutual validation, even sometimes demonstrating considerable continuity. Perhaps the clearest example of this is how we are compelled to retell the history of "environmental justice" activism (supposedly born from a sharp break with mainstream environmentalism in the 1980s and 1990s) by connecting it to a longstanding, rich tradition of similarly militant protest. That tradition likewise linked environmental problems to economic inequality and ethnic and racial marginalization, emphasized grassroots community organizing in the face of corporate and government intransigence, and occasionally employed nonviolent civil disobedience as well as armed self-defense.

Finally, it should be noted that a revisionist interpretation of American environmentalism would not be possible without a steady stream of other pioneering scholarly books and articles published over the last decade and a half (or more). Taken together, they point toward a broader, more inclusive, more empowering narrative of American environmentalism. As often as possible, in relevant sections, *The Myth of "Silent Spring"* acknowledges individual historians for their contributions, crediting them for venturing into uncharted territory and reconfiguring the shape of the larger story (like John Cumbler and his *Reasonable Use*) or returning to well-worked ground and uncovering fresh insights (like Elizabeth Blum and her *Love Canal Revisited*). For readers who want to explore a particular topic or theme in greater depth, the book includes a final section, "Further Reading," with an abbreviated list of sources that were most useful to me in developing the ideas presented here.

CHAPTER ONE

"I Think Less of the Factory Than of My Native Dell"

Perhaps to ease readers into the parade of difficult concepts and scientific formulas that fill the rest of the book, Rachel Carson began *Silent Spring* with a short fable. The setting was a town "in the heart of America," nestled among "a checkerboard of prosperous farms," a wondrous place where "all life seemed to live in harmony with its surroundings." Orchards bloomed white in the spring, forest trees blazed brilliant colors in the fall, wildflowers and ferns lined roadsides, foxes and deer roamed the land half hidden in morning mists, birds fed on berries and seeds, and streams full of trout ran cold and clear. Then one day everything started to sicken and die and the world went quiet. In the gutters, under the eaves, and between the shingles of the roofs was a white granular powder that had come from the sky some weeks before, falling "like snow." Carson left the powder (like the town) unnamed, but her modern telling of a biblical fall from grace was clearly both an explanation and a warning. "A grim specter has crept upon us almost unnoticed," she wrote, and "this imagined tragedy may easily become a stark reality we all shall know."[1]

In *Silent Spring's* much longer second chapter that followed the fable Carson presented a history of how science had brought humanity to the brink of calamity. "Only within the moment of time represented by the present century," she noted, has our own species "acquired significant power to alter the nature of this world." And in the quarter century just passed this power had increased in magnitude and changed in character, reaching a whole new scale and acquiring a previously unconceivable potency. "The most alarming of all man's assaults upon the environment," Carson explained, "is the contamination of air, earth, rivers, and sea with dangerous and even lethal materials." The two most ominous were chemicals ("sprayed on croplands or forests or gardens") and radiation ("released through nuclear explosions into the air"). Both were legacies of World War II, the one greatly aided by chemical weapons research and the other a product of atomic and nuclear weapons testing. Together they posed an unprecedented threat to the "adjustment" and "balance" that life had reached with its surroundings over hundreds of millions of years. "The rapidity of change and the speed with which new situations are created," Carson pointed out, "follow the impetuous and heedless pace of man rather than the deliberate pace of nature."[2]

There is, of course, some truth in these initial observations and claims. By the time Rachel Caron sat down to write what was going to be her third and last book, human ingenuity had indeed managed to introduce a whole new set of environmental threats to our well-being and safety (ironically in the name of feeding and protecting us), and people were only just beginning to become aware of how serious those particular threats might be. Yet by opening *Silent Spring* the way she did, casting ruinous environmental change as a uniquely mid-twentieth-century phenome-

non, Carson misinterpreted history, relying on an inventive portrait of the past to make her jeremiad seem even more timely and
necessary (as any compelling jeremiad has to be). Apparently this
was convincing, persuading many that the book had an importance that went beyond its summary of the dangers pesticides
posed and inspiring them to proclaim that *Silent Spring* was the
"start of it all"—even though they were slightly, if not significantly, mistaken. Profound environmental transformation by
humankind was hardly new. Different human cultures in various
places had been causing "changes on the land" for eons, doing
what virtually defines us as a species. And the particular problems
that gave rise to a modern American environmental movement
began more than a century earlier (at least), with the onset of
industrialization and its many attendant consequences.

The first mills and factories in the United States, built in the
decades prior to the Civil War, disturbed the ecology of agrar-
ian life in various ways, namely by erecting ever-higher permanent dams on local streams and rivers and filling those same
waterways with all manner of filth. The dams were necessary to
harness water power that turned intricate belt systems hooked
up to machines, but the mill ponds they created flooded river
meadows that farmers used to feed their cattle, while the actual
structures blocked migratory fish that many relied on as a food
source. In decades past, most grain mill and sawmill operators
lowered their dams or raised passage gates at different times of
the year to let freshets through and allow rich silt to nourish
meadow grass, and if the gates were not sufficient they constructed "fishways" to allow alewife, shad, salmon, and other
anadromous fish to pass upstream. Textile mills and other manufacturers did not operate their dams in this manner, however,
and they caused additional problems by daily dumping millions

of gallons of noxious waste into streams and rivers. There it mixed with untreated sewage and other household waste from residents in growing cities, the places where new industrial workers came to live. As a result, by the end of the nineteenth century many waterways were not only blocked but also profoundly unsightly, terribly smelly, and, because they were often the source of water for drinking and other domestic uses, the likely cause of regular, deadly epidemics.

Responses to the environmental harm done by manufacturing were wide-ranging, and they began what would become a tradition of popular environmental protest in the United States. Using a long-held right recognized under common law, some local farmers busted up offending milldams, at first without attempting to hide their deeds and eventually, as states passed new laws that made such destruction a criminal act, working under the cover of night. Ordinary country people and town dwellers filed lawsuits against corporations as well, drawing on a shared understanding of riparian law that allowed only certain "reasonable" use. Over the course of the nineteenth century, however, courts and state legislatures sided more and more often with private industry, establishing manufacturing as the favored use for its supposedly superior contribution to the common good. Meanwhile, early public health advocates complemented the direct action and court challenges by creating city and state boards of health, justifying this new state intervention with an expansive interpretation of the natural rights enshrined by the American Revolution, one that included the guarantee of clean water and air. The boards collected statistics, oversaw municipal sanitation, and incrementally acquired powers to prevent or at least control pollution (which, by the early twentieth century, included smoke in the air as well as waste in waterways), yet they too were not infrequently blocked by influential industrial interests.

In fact, by the turn of the next century, most state and federal government involvement in regulating the environmental impact of industrialization bore the heavy imprint of America's hardening social divisions and unequal distribution of power. Newly created state and regional fish commissions did their part for fish restoration, propagating fish and restocking streams and rivers, but they focused less on species best suited as a food source and more on "game fishes" desired by "gentlemen anglers." Similarly, game commissions began to impose rules and regulations on hunting designed to please the ranks of elite sport hunters, usually at the expense of those who relied on game for subsistence and despite the fact that most communities already had well-understood and effective rules governing when and how they hunted and what they hunted for. This was the case with early forest conservation agencies as well, which stopped generally sustainable local harvesting of timber in order to maintain the timber resources needed to ensure corporate wealth and aid the country's incipient imperial aspirations. Meanwhile, those seeking to protect so-called wilderness from any human use relied on federal troops to remove and keep out Native Americans and white settlers from the first national parks. These and other uses of government power were grounded in a widespread belief among white elites that those among the lower social classes and assumed inferior races could not and would not reliably support efforts to protect wild areas, conserve natural resources, or reduce pollution. Subsequently, the drive to impose a narrow version of conservation and preservation in place of the "moral ecology" of common people set up an enduring conflict that was not settled for several more decades.

"NO GRASS, NO MANURE; NO MANURE, NO CATTLE; NO CATTLE, NO CROPS"

In 1708, the town of Billerica, Massachusetts, granted a mill privilege to Christopher Osgood, allowing him to construct a milldam at Billerica Falls, on the Concord River. Residents living upstream, in Concord and Sudbury, did not look kindly on this, since the structure interfered with their own use of the waterway and adjacent land, and they persuaded the commission of sewers to order Osgood to remove the dam. When he refused to do so, the aggrieved inhabitants petitioned the General Court in Boston, working under the assumption that any water use was supposed to allow water to flow "as it customarily flowed" and not do damage to others. "The Fish have been almost wholly Obstructed from passing up," they explained, "and a Great Quantity of their land Laid under Water." The court agreed with the commission and petitioners, and in 1722 the dam was either torn down or at least lowered far enough to keep the water from backing up on the distant farmers' meadows, and no new complaints were recorded.[3] Presumably, the flooded land was what bothered the petitioners most, more than the way the dam impeded fish runs, and that was because the type of farming they did only worked if there was an ample source of meadow grass. Adapting the mixed husbandry of East Anglia, where the original Puritan settlers hailed from, eighteenth-century farmers cut hay to feed to cattle that made manure, which was used to maintain soil fertility in the fields, succinctly described in a common saying, "No grass, no manure; no manure, no cattle; no cattle, no crops." Obstructions on local waterways that were high enough and kept in place year round interfered with summer mowing, disrupting the cycle.[4]

What makes the dispute about Osgood's dam particularly interesting is that it shows how eighteenth-century farmers believed they had the law on their side—which they did. For a while, they even had the right to remove obstructions themselves. If a dam was seen as a common nuisance, the Massachusetts supreme court had ruled that "any individual of their private authority might tear it down at any season." So in 1799, after Joseph Ruggle raised his milldam on a stream that ran into the Connecticut River, in the western part of the state, flooding fifty acres of land, Elijah Boardman and some of his friends ripped out the new upper portion. Decades later, this was still common practice. In 1827, Oliver Mosley and a dozen others tore down Horace White's milldam on the Agawam River, near Plymouth.[5] Farther north, in the lakes region of New Hampshire, dam breaking was even more widespread, and because the legislature there was slower to outlaw the practice, it went on for much longer. Tensions were probably at their highest at midcentury, as Boston investors gained control over the state's largest lakes and systematically dammed the outflowing rivers, to ensure adequate water flow to their factories downstream in Lowell and Lawrence. In one case, in 1859, when the dam at Folsom Falls in Lake Village caused his land to flood, George Young took an iron bar to the structure, though without much effect. He returned with a group of men and they proceeded to pull off planks until company agents forcibly stopped them. After nightfall, fifty local farmers came back with a sheriff, who arrested the agents for assault and battery while the crowd went at the dam again, "with axes and bars," although again without success. Considering the difficulty of simple dismantlement, when another aggrieved group wanted to take down the Amoskeag Manufacturing Company's dam in Manchester, on the Merrimack River, they tried to blow it up, but a watchman found the flask of gunpowder and disconnected the fuse.[6]

Eventually, as the industrial revolution swept across New England, legislatures and courts remade riparian (water) law to favor corporate manufacturers over any other users. At first in Massachusetts, legislators attempted to resolve conflicts between farmers and milldam operators with "mill acts," which provided for juries to determine compensation to landowners when a dam flooded meadows and fields. The law they passed in 1796 took away the right of dam breaking and made compensation the exclusive remedy, capped the damages, allowed for an annual adjustment of the amount, and meanwhile permitted the obstruction to remain, making mill owners tenants of flooded land on very favorable terms. Several times during the next century, as large textile mills, paper manufacturers, tanneries, and machine shops replaced small carding mills, sawmills, and gristmills, the state supreme court endorsed this accommodation on water rights. "In consideration of the advantage to the public to be derived from the establishment and maintenance of mills," Chief Justice Samuel Shaw declared in 1851, "the owner of the land shall not have an action for their necessary consequential damage against the mill owner, to compel him to ... destroy or reduce his head of water."[7]

Two years later, in a case before the Massachusetts state supreme court, the Essex Company argued that its act of incorporation allowed it to ignore a county requirement to maintain a fishway on their huge dam in Lawrence and, more generally, to damage private property by eminent domain, claiming that textile manufacturing was a greater public use than any other. The justices agreed. Similarly, in New Hampshire in 1868, the legislature finally passed a mill act of its own that effectively transferred control over rivers and streams to private corporations.

The law empowered the supreme court to appoint a committee to investigate damage claims, and if the committee determined the obstruction to be "of public use or benefits to the people of this state," it would estimate the amount for compensation while flooded land stayed under water.[8]

Industrialization was advancing at such a rapid pace in New England that by the time the famed Concord native Henry David Thoreau hopped in a boat with his brother John for an excursion down the Concord River, just before midcentury, he could already see plenty of evidence that a profound transformation of the natural landscape was taking place. There was a new dam at Billerica Falls, three feet higher than the one Osgood built a hundred years before, intended to divert water into the newly constructed Middlesex Canal, flooding upstream meadows for many miles. There were also numerous textile mills, an iron works, a leather tannery, and other manufacturing along the banks downstream from that point, with dams at Massic Falls and Middlesex Falls, all the way to the confluence with the Merrimack River in Lowell. And one more register of the larger change under way, an environmental consequence of industrialization, was the nearly complete lack of anadromous fish. "Salmon, shad, and Alewives were formerly abundant here," Thoreau later wrote in a book about the trip, "taken in weirs by the Indians, who taught this method to the whites, by whom they were used as food and as manure, until the dam, and afterward the canal at Billerica, and the factories at Lowell, put an end to their migration hither-afterward." There were more dams, they were bigger, they were no longer left open for the seasonal migration, and fishways were not properly constructed. "Poor shad," he bemoaned, "Where is thy redress?" In this moment of transition there seemed to be not much anyone could do, although Thoreau (like many of his neighbors) knew this was not always the case. "I for one am with thee," he declared, "and who knows what may avail a crow-bar against that Billerica dam?"[9]

"LIKE A PRISONED BIRD"

For those coming to work in the new mills and factories from homesteads in the distant countryside, the environmental change happening along New England waterways was shocking, while the new life they led also dramatically altered their own relationship with nature. Most of the first textile mill operatives were young, single women, sent off by their families to earn a cash wage. They were used to organizing their days according to natural rhythms: the rising and setting of the sun, the needs of livestock, as well as vagaries of weather and seasonal cycles, which determined what might be planted, harvested, gathered, picked, logged, tapped, or hunted. The labor was sometimes arduous and even monotonous, yet individual members of a farm family could often set their own pace, vary their activities through the day or week, and intermix meaningful interactions with a spouse, parents, siblings, neighbors, and others. They had a chance to be both indoors and outdoors as well, fishing for trout, collecting herbs, selling eggs, and doing other errands. In the mills, however, the workday was ordered by hourly bells and impersonal overseers. Indifferent machines established the work pace, labor was typically dull, repetitive, and unchanging throughout the year, and work rooms were often oppressively hot and noisy. When their day was done, operatives went home to crowded boarding houses or filthy tenement districts, with inadequate or nonexistent street cleaning and waste collection, seeing flowers, trees, and birds only when they walked on a town common, visited a "garden" cemetery, or took a trip away. "Nature" was no longer something the young women knew directly, through meaningful labor and normal family life, but as something apart from their ordinary existence, "out there," a place to encounter passively.

As mill hands grew disillusioned with the way their labor separated them from the natural world, the more literary-minded among them began to invent and express a "romantic" outlook about nature. Back at their homestead, writing in diaries or later writing a memoir about their farming days, they often observed beauty and even spiritual significance in the surrounding landscape, but mostly they characterized it by use. Living in factory towns, the women were more inclined to notice and emphasize nature's metaphysical qualities or, at least, its moral symbolism, increasingly to the exclusion of its utilitarian features. "It is not possible to hear the sweet music of the birds, warbling forth their notes from every bough," one operative explained, "without feeling the mind impressed with a sense of the wisdom of our Creator, and conceiving pleasures and delights unlike and far purer than can be gained or conceived of in the crowd and noise of the city."[10] This was not too different from the transcendentalism that various writers were working out at the same time in Concord, Massachusetts, a philosophy that insisted on the natural world's correspondence to spiritual truths and looked warily at cities and their industry for defiling the rivers, forests, and meadows brimful with the "universal soul." Ralph Waldo Emerson boldly announced those ideas in his book *Nature,* published in 1836, and his younger acquaintance Henry David Thoreau expounded on something like them in his own writing. Yet in contrast to these more comfortably perched men (even during the two years Thoreau lived in the woods at Walden Pond he was hardly a rustic), the operatives' observations and notions originated from direct experience with

the machines and a materialism that the transcendentalists bemoaned only from a distance.

Oddly, considering the consistently negative tenor of their
thoughts and opinions, a good portion of the mill commentary
was published in company-supported literary journals, part of
an early attempt by manufacturers to demonstrate that American industrial capitalism was culturally as well as materially
uplifting and far from Britain's infamous "dark satanic mills." In
one piece, published in the *Operatives' Magazine* in 1841, a worker
using the initials V.C.N. described an early-morning walk she
took along the Merrimack River, filling her with rapture before
the workday began. The river "carelessly rolled" and sent "its
tranquil waters to mingle with the great deep," and while sitting
and musing on her surroundings, the young woman "was led to
think upon the Creator of them all." Then, however, she was
"roused by the pealing tones of the bell which told me that I was
wanted" and she walked back to the city "where, as usual, all was
noise and bustle," although the "calmness and serenity" gained
from the excursion was "not easily effaced."[11]

Similarly, operatives wrote about their confinement "in the
massey brick walls of a hateful factory" and intense longing
for the natural world beyond it.[12] In a *Lowell Offering* essay, "A
Weaver's Reverie," Harriet Farley recounted leaving "the cir-
cumscribed spot which is my appointed place of labor, that I
might look from an adjoining window upon the bright loveliness
of nature," feeling her heart flutter "like a prisoned bird, with its
painful longings for an unchecked flight amid the beautiful creation around me." A friend had recently asked her why "the factory girls write so much about the beauties of nature," and Farley had explained that it was because an operative's lot was so far
removed from them, limited to "the crowded clattering mill,"

"the noisy tenement which is her home," and "the thronged and busy street which she may sometimes tread."[13]

In fact, mill girls routinely attempted brief excursions by stagecoach and train to the local countryside or, if they had more time, to distant family homesteads, again juxtaposing what they objected to about factory work and city life with romantic observations about nature. "Those who have for any length of time been pent up in a cotton mill and factory boarding-house," one operative explained during a summer trip to Lebanon Springs, "can appreciate the pleasures of a journey through the country, when the earth is dressed in her richest roves of green, bedecked with flowers, and all smiling with sunlight." Musing on the meaning of the scenery, she insisted "that man had made the town, but God had made the country."[14] Likewise, writing to the workmates she left behind for a visit to her family home, J. R. assured them: "think not while surrounded by the green fields, feasting my mind with their beauties, that I do not cast a sympathizing thought to the many shut up in the mills, constantly toiling, without time to look abroad upon the face of nature and 'view the glorious handiworks of their Creator.'" Wandering the waterways that fed the Merrimack River and turned the factory belts in Lowell, she listened to birdsong and pondered "the evils growing up in the present state of society, which must undermine all glorious scenes with 'her thousand votaries of art.'"[15]

In between time away, or in later memoirs, young women also imagined the lost landscapes of their former lives, which they typically stripped of any reference to the considerable amount of work they once did there and took plenty of poetic license to otherwise embellish. Some operatives claimed these fanciful flights were the only thing that made the mills tolerable, although they seemed to stir their discontent and deepen their longing too. In one literary journal piece, "Recollections of My Childhood," Betsy Chamberlain, who grew up in Wolfesboro, New Hampshire, and later moved to New Market and then Lowell, recalled how she once waded the pond for lilies and the brooks for minnows, roamed the fields for berries and the meadows for flowers, wandered the woods for ivy-plums and watched the robins build their yearly nest in chestnut trees, and nursed "with truly motherly care" the early lambs and chickens.[16] In a song that apparently made the rounds of Britain as well as New England with varying substituted place references, "The Lowell Factory Girl," the singer at one point laments leaving her "native country" to be "summoned by the bell" and declares "I think less of the factory / Than of my native dell."[17]

Writing many decades after a stint in the mills, Lucy Larcom recalled growing up on a Cape Ann farm, admitting how she shirked the garden weeding her father sometimes sent the children to do, and "stole off into the shade of the great apple-tree, and let the west wind fan my hot cheeks, and looked up into the boughs, and listened to the many birds that seemed clattering to each other in a language of their own." When her father died, their mother moved the family to Lowell. Larcom eventually took a position as a spinner, and "the confinement of the mill became very wearisome," at times prompting her to lean far out the window, trying not to hear "the unceasing clash of sound inside," gazing toward the hills in the distance, her "whole being" crying out, "Oh that I had wings!"[18]

"A VERY OFFENSIVE STENCH"

Besides the common objections to mills and factories, the operatives' writing suggests that many antebellum Americans found fault with the conditions in industrial cities as well, especially as they grew in size and density and their problems worsened. Necessary municipal sanitation services and even the notion of public responsibility for city residents' health and well-being happened only after industrial manufacturing and the urban expansion it galvanized had been going on for some time. Consequently, throughout the nineteenth century and well into the twentieth city dwellers suffered streets filled with putrid garbage, water polluted by assorted factory waste and raw sewage, and (eventually) air heavy with noxious smoke from industrial smokestacks and domestic coal fires. These intolerable sanitary conditions were far from the "glorious handiworks of the creator," and they gave many an even greater appreciation for the pastoral countryside. But the conditions were also dangerous, the cause of common illness and death from certain endemic diseases and higher mortality rates from various epidemic diseases, and they spurred increasing numbers of individual complaints as well as mounting organized protest. A preponderance of those complaints and protests recognized the way social inequity factored into the mounting menace to public health and laid the blame for it on corporations. This social justice–minded concern with sanitation was, effectively, the beginning of widespread environmental consciousness and an important foundation for the American environmental movement.

Corporations located the first mills and factories along watercourses because they relied on waterpower, yet they also found the location convenient for disposing of the vast amount and array of manufacturing "waste liquors" and other refuse they produced. A medium-sized cotton textile mill, for example, annually flushed 600 million gallons of wastewater into nearby rivers or streams, a viscous amalgam laden with used dyes, such as madder, peachwood, logwood, and sumac, as well as spent chemicals, such as sulfuric acid, muriatic acid, soda ash, bleaching powder, lime, soap, and arsenate of soda. The effluent from pulp production at a typical paper mill included remainders from boiling rags in caustic lime (releasing dirt, grease, and dyes), combining suspended fiber with alum or sulfuric acid and bleaching it in chloride of lime, and then mixing that with alum, soda, resin, and clay, while making pulp from wood, which became more common in the second half of the nineteenth century, generated even nastier pollutants. Tanneries turned "green hides" into finished leather by scraping and washing them clean of dirt, manure, blood, fat, and hair, soaking them in a vat of water, salt, and chicken manure (to make them more pliable), and tanning them in pits of a bark and water "ooze," each step making solid and liquid waste that was unceremoniously dumped into an adjacent waterway. And metalworking (increasingly important for fabricating the machines that other factories used) contributed to the outflow as well, specifically burnt particulates (cinders, scoriae, and furnace ashes), acids, and metallic salts.[19]

Along with production wastes, mills and factories maintained privies for workers that put raw sewage directly or indirectly into local brooks and rivers. In New Britain, Connecticut, by the second half of the nineteenth century there were more than three thousand operatives engaged in iron, brass, hardware, wool, and cotton manufacturing, and the workplace privies they used drained into Piper's Brook, fouling the stream with 2,500 pounds of feces and 3,500 gallons of urine a day. According to farmers living downstream, this gave the brook's water a "very disagreeable stench," rendered it "wholly unfit for the use of cattle," killed what fish it once accommodated, and spread "typho-malarial fever."[20] Chicopee, Massachusetts, had three times as many workers, among 18 cotton mills, 33 foundries, 26 woolen mills and dye works, 3 paper mills, 6 gas works, a bleaching works, a hat works, 3 tanneries, and 34 sawmills and gristmills, each of which maintained numerous water closets or outhouses that emptied into ditches that dumped into the Chicopee or the Connecticut River, likewise creating "a very offensive stench."[21] Additionally, the many privy vaults and cesspools serving company-owned boardinghouses and private tenements in quickly growing manufacturing towns overflowed with yet more human sewage and household waste, seeping out when full to drain into streams or more often to form mucky puddles. "Sewerage and drainage are in a very imperfect condition in many parts of the city," physician Josiah Curtis declared in his survey of midcentury Lowell, "and many lanes and alleys are without either[,] the house-slops and other refuses remaining on the surface, especially in wet weather." This too "impregnated the air" with "effluvia" and filled whole neighborhoods with "noxious exhalations."[22]

The specific concern public health advocates and various others voiced about bad odors in urban industrial towns was rooted in the era's prevailing understanding of disease etiology—what caused illnesses like typhoid, cholera, and dysentery. Until the end of the nineteenth century and even into the first decade of the twentieth, many people thought that most if not all diseases were acquired by inhaling "miasmas" or smelly gases emanating from decaying or moldering filth, natural or otherwise, and the more something smelled, the more dangerous it was likely to be to human health. To be sure, a few scientists and medical professionals believed that the bad odors indicated the airborne presence of invisible "fomites," anticipating the work of Robert Koch and Louis Pasteur decades later that identified the actual microorganisms responsible, individual viruses and bacteria that had their own specific ways of getting into the human body. Yet the miasmatic theory of disease tended to draw attention not to the infectious agents but rather to the noxious waste that was putrefying and releasing them (whatever they were) into the air. This partly (though not wholly) erroneous perspective eventually became the basis for a sanitary movement that devised and implemented effective urban environmental reform measures, lessening the presence of diseases and lowering mortality rates even before anyone had a correct notion about why and how they happened.

The partly confused understanding of disease etiology was already at play in the early part of 1799, when Elijah Boardman and other residents of New Milford, Connecticut, destroyed part of a milldam owned by Joseph Ruggles, a structure that stretched across the Housatonic River and "nearly opposite the most compact part of town." Like other dam breakers of the time, the men freely admitted what they did and justified the act by claiming the dam in question was a public nuisance, "the cause of distressing sickness, which had for several years visited New-Milford." After Ruggles had raised the structure's height by ten inches three years earlier, the area was struck by "a bilious remitting fever," a sickness that Boardman and the rest attributed to the effluvia coming from "much stagnant water" in a low marshy area behind it. When the milldam owner took the culprits to court, suing them for unlawful damage to his property, the defendants called several "medical gentlemen" as witnesses, all of whom generally agreed "that the bilious remitting fever, and fever and ague, of our country, are produced by marsh effluvia, [and] that this effluvia is caused by animal and vegetable putrefaction." Members of the jury accepted this notion, but they were divided about whether the pool of stagnant water made by the dam was strictly responsible for New Milford's epidemic. So they decided in favor of Ruggles.[23]

After the turn of the century, when corporations newly built or raised milldams to generate waterpower for manufacturing that also put loads of industrial waste and privy contents into waterways, residents in towns scattered about New England made an increasing numbers of complaints about the stench of putrefying filth (and not just the odorous stagnant water the dams created). Mr. L. S. Wells, who lived downstream from New Britain, Connecticut, on Piper's Brook, complained of "a distinct odor in summer season as well as in winter" and said his cows were sickened from drinking the water. Another local resident reported that two farmers who lived near the brook had recently died of "typho-malarial fever," pointing to the factories and mills upstream as the source. Sometimes, in fact, these public objections explicitly recognized the ways in which "changes on the land" that were possibly causing harm to livestock and human health were intertwined with social, economic, and political change shifting greater power toward corporations. Speaking before the Agricultural Board of Connecticut in 1886, for example, farmer James Olcott called on his audience and "the common people" of the state to "agitate" against "polluted streams," particularly the "sewage from families and factories, festering in every pool and mill pond—formerly trout holes." It was "ignorant or reckless capitalists" who caused this "social evil," he said, and public action would be necessary to "bring lasting welfare to the whole commonwealth."[24]

"IT IS CERTAINLY THE DUTY OF THE GOVERNMENT TO PROTECT THE WEAK FROM OPPRESSION OF THE STRONG"

In the mid-nineteenth century, at least in New England, it was newly created state boards of health that took the leading public role against industrial pollution and urban sanitation problems. The Massachusetts board, the first established and the most militant, was chaired by Henry Ingersoll Bowditch, a professor of clinical medicine at the Harvard School of Medicine, vice president of the American Medical Association, and a radical abolitionist, women's rights advocate, and housing reformer, who believed the state should guarantee that each citizen "not only have as long a life as nature would give him, but live as healthy a life as possible." He made the case for what he called "state medicine" by reinterpreting the natural rights claims embedded in the Declaration of Independence. The original document insisted that the rights to life, liberty, and the pursuit of happiness were inherent and inalienable to all, and if government failed to protect those rights, people also had the right to alter or even abolish it. With the advent of industrial manufacturing, driven by private capital, Bowditch insisted that government responsibilities and powers had to evolve too.[25]

"We believe that every person has a legitimate right to nature's gifts, pure water, air, and soil," the Massachusetts board declared in its first annual report, in 1869, "a right belonging to every individual and every community, upon which no one should be allowed to trespass through carelessness, ignorance, or other cause." A few years later, New Hampshire's state board used the exact same language in its first annual report as well, while the Connecticut board went a step further with more explicit acknowledgment of social divisions and inequity. "It is certainly the duty of the government to protect the weak from oppression of the strong," the members declared in their second annual report, in 1879, "and especially to protect the class called the poor." That class suffered the most from "unwholesome surroundings and other unsanitary conditions," they said, though it was "only a question of time how long it will be before each state ... must provide some official means to also protect the public at large."[26]

Not surprisingly, the influence of state health boards waxed and waned as corporations attempted to defend their expanding rights to alter and affect the region's landscape, just as they fought the labor movement's efforts to limit manufacturers' license to exploit workers. The struggle was especially dramatic and drawn out in Massachusetts, where Bowditch and other outspoken and persistent public health crusaders were making noticeable headway. Under his leadership, they successfully pressured the state legislature to pass an "Act Relative to the Pollution of Rivers, Streams, and Ponds," which prohibited the discharge of municipal sewage and industrial waste near a public water supply. The law exempted some polluters by prescription or long-standing use, however, as well as those on the most industrial rivers, the Connecticut and Merrimack and the short section of the Concord that passed through Lowell.[27]

Not taking any chances, soon after the pollution law's enactment manufacturers convinced the governor to merge the board of health with the boards of lunacy and charity, both chaired by corporate lawyer Charles Francis Donnelly, who took over the merged board, prompting Bowditch to resign. The new board, he complained, had fallen "into the hands of self seeking capitalists who were afraid of the millstreams being cleaned." Democrat Benjamin Butler replaced Donnelly with activist Henry

Walcott when he became governor, but in 1883 Butler lost his bid for reelection to Republican George Robinson, who put Donnelly back in charge. After a series of newspaper stories and a lobbying campaign, Robinson reestablished an independent board of health and made Walcott the chair, after which, in 1886, the state legislature passed another water quality bill. The new law charged the board with "the general oversight and care of all inland waters" and funded a pioneering experiment station to investigate the best methods for treating sewage and cleaning water. The next year, even before the station was organized, the state funded what turned out to be a historic sewage and water quality survey as well.[28]

Part of what made the sanitary survey historic is that it was overseen and conducted primarily by Ellen Swallow Richards, the first woman to be admitted to the Massachusetts Institute of Technology (MIT), where she earned her B.S. in 1873, and the first woman to teach there, starting at an auxiliary Women's Laboratory where female students attended apart from male students. After the school integrated women and men in 1884 and the auxiliary lab was closed and razed, Richards served briefly in an advisory capacity at a new Sanitary Chemistry Laboratory and eventually received an official appointment to the faculty. By all accounts, she was an expert chemist and renowned mineralogist, and when MIT hired William Sedgwick, the two of them collaborated to turn the various life sciences courses into a full-fledged biology program. By then Richards not only had a firm grasp of a range of scientific disciplines but also a portentous understanding of how they fit together. The sanitary survey, which she did in collaboration with another new MIT faculty member, Thomas Messinger Drown, gave Richards a chance to test and apply this comprehensive knowledge and convinced her to adopt the term "oekology," coined by one of her many international correspondents, Ernst Haeckel. The work itself, including her own analysis of more than forty thousand water samples, produced the world's first water purity tables and established the first state water quality standards in the United States, although Drown received official credit for the results. Undeterred by the slight, Richards created the first "Sanitary Engineering" course, a combination of chemistry, bacteriology, and engineering, one that was critical to training the students who went on to staff the experiment station.[29]

The newly reconstituted Massachusetts state board of health had included two "reformers" and two manufacturers' representatives as well as Hiram Mills, the chief engineer for the Essex Company in Lawrence. Mills was already operating a hydraulic experiment station to study more efficient ways to draw power from the local canals, and with the addition of a laboratory building that facility became the site for the new sanitary station, located at the confluence of the Merrimack and Spicket rivers. In an official history later published by the board, the so-called Father of American Sanitary Engineering was the person credited with bringing together the various scientific and engineering talent there, but it was actually Ellen Swallow Richards who played the leading part, recruiting and coordinating the work of the otherwise all-male staff. Sedgwick, whom she helped become a bacteriologist, spent some time at the station in its early years, as did her water quality study collaborator Drown and her students Edwin O. Jordan, Allen Hazen, and C.-E. A. Winslow, each of whom went on to receive wide acclaim.[30]

In any case, the experiments these scientists conducted were critical to developing modern techniques for purifying water and treating sewage as well as advancing the notion that the state could and should do this for the protection of public health. They were also part of a larger shift toward acceptance of the germ theory, since they started from the premise that microscopic pathogens were responsible for disease and the various investigations into filtration, aeration, and coagulation were meant to remove those particular microbes. After a typhoid epidemic swept through the Merrimack River valley in the early 1890s, Lawrence began to clean some of its water with slow sand filters, and when this proved effective, in 1907 they added more filter beds to the plant, with a capacity to clean 3 million gallons per acre a day, making it the first city in the country to filter its entire water supply for disease prevention. For the most part, however, Lawrence Experiment Station investigations emphasized engineering solutions over prevention, and what little attention the staff gave to industrial waste was limited to treating with chemicals.[31]

"TAKE SUCH STEPS AND MEASURES AS WELL IN THEIR JUDGMENT"

The rapidly industrializing New England states addressed the sharp decline in migratory fish populations much as they dealt with waterborne disease, overlooking the proliferation of immense dams and noxious pollution that were the actual causes of failing fish runs and assuming the possibility of a technical fix. In Lawrence, for example, the 900-foot-long, 35-foot-high Great Stone Dam that powered the city's mills was an insurmountable obstacle for fish attempting to go upstream, while water fouled by printing and dyeing at the city's mills posed an additional threat to them. The Pacific Mills used "fourfold more dyes and chemicals than do all the other factories in the place put together," a report by scientists Theodore Lyman and Louis Aggasiz explained, and the waste from that company was the primary reason for the disappearance of the once bountiful shad fishery below the dam by the end of the 1850s.[32] But nuisance suits were no longer effective for residents to get redress in cases like these, since courts were more and more tending to favor the supposed "public good" provided by manufacturing over the interests the public might have in clear and clean waterways. Likewise, while state legislators depended on common people for votes, they were more often swayed by the organized influence of private capital, as the limited laws they passed in response to decimation of fisheries clearly reflected. The various measures focused official attention and public resources on building fishways (or fish ladders) to get fish over the dams and on establishing fry hatcheries to raise fish for restocking waterways, both solutions that would not threaten continued corporate profitability.

Responding to complaints from residents and their representatives in New Hampshire and Vermont, the Massachusetts General Court passed the first fish act, "Concerning the Obstruction to the Passage of Fish in the Connecticut and Merrimack Rivers," in the spring of 1866. The law established a permanent fish commission to begin planning for fishways and funded the first fish hatchery. Connecticut established its own fish commission later that same year, enabling the two states to work together, and then, in 1867, conservationists created the New England Commission of River Fisheries. This was important recognition that the problem was a regional one, requiring not only unprecedented state intervention but also a new kind of interstate cooperation.[33]

Yet the steps forward stopped there. When reformer Theodore Lyman suggested that a new Massachusetts fish act should increase government power to prevent or limit pollution—prohibiting waste disposal in streams and rivers but allowing an exception if there was no reasonable alternative—mill owners and their supporters in the legislature roundly rejected the idea. Additionally, as it turned out, the fishways generally failed to get shad, salmon, alewives, and eels upstream, and this put the burden of fish restoration on restocking by hatcheries.[34] The hatcheries, however, decided to focus on raising the fish desired by a new constituency of elite sport fishermen, rather than those species that yeoman farmers and common operatives wanted for food. "Sometimes it has been charged by those who have not given the subject careful consideration," the Massachusetts commissioners said in their defense, "that this commission is largely engaged in propagating game fishes for the few at the expense of the many." In fact, they were. "It should be taken into consideration that the so called game fishes are the highest order of fishes, and that the love of angling is on the increase," they explained, and "the whole people must be considered in the matter of propagating and planting fish in the waters of the state."[35]

The New England fish commissions' growing concern with managing fish in the interest of sportsmen was only the beginning of a larger turn toward monitoring and controlling other natural resources for the elite more generally and widely, eventually encompassing game, timber, and "wilderness" throughout the Northeast and the rest of the country. Typically this was done by state commissions and federal agencies on the basis of the ostensibly "scientific" policies they crafted and imposed, policies that turned traditional uses of ordinary people into crimes. "For many rural communities," historian Karl Jacoby explains, "the most notable feature of conservation was the transformation of previously acceptable practices into illegal acts: hunting or fishing redefined as poaching, foraging as trespassing, the setting of fires as arson, and the cutting of trees as timber theft." Their reaction, understandably, was hostile, even rising to the level of "environmental banditry," community-sanctioned violations of restrictions and regulations that included willful disregard of the rules, threats and violence toward those given the task of enforcement, and collusion among local residents to protect lawbreakers from punishment. Crusading conservationists made sense of the banditry, Jacoby notes, by painting the outlaws as inherently malicious and too ignorant to recognize their own flawed understanding of the natural world, sentiment usually complemented by some variant and combination of racism, ethnic prejudice, and class arrogance.[36]

What conservation advocates and government agents missed was the complex "moral ecology" that residents in many communities had developed over a long period of time, a set of standards and expectations, often socially equitable and environmentally sound, that enabled them to practice collective restraint in the use of forests, fields, and streams. In some cases, these rules were explicit, written, and enforced with official authority. In 1840, for example, the people of Goldsborough, Maine, petitioned the state legislature to allow for creating a local fish committee that would meet and discuss removing dams or other obstructions and "take such Steps & measures as well in their judgment" that would allow fish to migrate upstream into Forbes Pond, and the legislature granted this right to them. Typically, however, the rules were unwritten and enforced without a formalized structure, followed partly because they made sense and seemed fair and partly because would-be violators faced real consequences, ranging from ridicule and snubbing (both particularly uncomfortable in a small village) to wrecked boats, killed dogs, and physical assaults. Moreover, it was not true that common people were wholly opposed to all state or federal conservation policies, even when they were made by largely unaccountable bureaucracies and administered in despotic ways by outsiders. They were especially willing to aid game wardens and forest rangers to deal with other outsiders—ill-mannered "gentlemen" sportsmen, rogue logging companies, and the like—who passed through communities and abided by neither local standards nor state and federal rules. Also, when rural dwellers moved to cities and became industrial wage laborers, their relationship with nature changed, they began to adopt hunting and fishing for recreation (rather than subsistence), and they acquired a new appreciation for government management of natural resources.[37]

"RIGHTS IN THE WOODS"

One of the earliest attempts to "conserve" natural resources that provoked intense local hostility happened during the late nineteenth century in the Adirondack region of upstate New York. In his celebrated book *Man and Nature,* published in 1864, George Perkins Marsh had warned of catastrophic ecological consequences if the rural populace there was allowed to continue their "unwise" use of the land and called on the state government to impose "scientific management." Subsequently, sport hunters seeking to protect the area as a hunting ground and manufacturers concerned about water flow to the canals feeding their mills and factories (often these were the same people) lobbied their state representatives. Then, in 1885, New York enacted a bill creating a forest preserve, which in 1892 became the centerpiece of a much larger state park. At the same time, the legislature passed restrictive game, timber, and fire laws and created a "forest police" empowered to arrest suspected violators without a warrant.[38]

Early reports from the Adirondack region indicated widespread disregard for the new policies—"utmost lawlessness" as one commission noted, though this was not quite accurate. People did attempt to resist in a variety of ways. They destroyed blazed trees and other monuments surveyors made to establish the park boundaries (allowing them to claim unintentional trespass); they tracked, threatened, and harassed foresters (some of whom were from mountain villages in the areas they patrolled and so already had divided loyalties); and they refused to cooperate in efforts to identify, catch, or prosecute violators (oftentimes their neighbors). Yet the "rights in the woods," a widely shared code allowing free access to undeveloped state and private lands for hunting, fishing, and foraging, included certain conventions limiting those forays. This included a prohibition against hunting deer when they were "yarding" or killing songbirds when they were nesting and an understanding that people would not take more than they needed.[39]

In fact, even more intolerable to Adirondack residents than restrictions on public lands was the increasing number of private parks, created by wealthy sportsmen and policed by hired guards, completely closing off some of the best hunting and fishing areas to everyone else. By 1893, there were sixty-three of these parks, totaling nearly a million acres. "The poor, as well as the men of moderate means, are complaining that our forest lands are rapidly being bought up by private clubs, and are closely watched by alert game keepers," the state legislature reported at the turn of the century, "and thus, as they claim, and not without some reason, our [woods] are all being monopolized by the rich; that we are apeing the English plan of barring the poor man from the hunt, etc." Tensions came to a violent head in 1903, when someone (never caught) shot and killed estate owner Orrando Dexter as he drove his carriage down a once-public road that he had enclosed, one of several things he had done to stop "trespassing." In the wake of the murder, other wealthy landowners hired more guards while locals stepped up acts of sabotage, ripping down "No Trespassing" signs, cutting wire fences, setting fires, and shooting at private parkland patrols. They also rallied to defend anyone who they thought was being unjustly punished. When William Rockefeller took Brandon resident Oliver Lamora to court, for instance, after his guard Fred Knapp caught Lamora fishing on Rockefeller's land once again, the case dragged on for four years. A jury finally awarded damages of only eighteen cents, while the community took up a subscription to help cover court costs. A couple of years later, some of Lamora's friends aided in the arrest and prosecution of John Redwood, Rockefeller's park superintendent, and Harry Melville, one of his gamekeepers, for hounding deer (prohibited by New York game laws), and they were fined one hundred dollars each.[40]

Farther out west, the conservation battle came to northeastern Minnesota with the creation of Superior National Forest in 1909. This was part of a larger federal effort to regulate timber extraction, which logging companies wanted as a means of ensuring future profits and which many American political leaders desired to maintain the resources needed for an expanding empire. Congress passed a Forest Reserve Act in 1891, and the U.S. Forest Service was established in 1905, followed several years later by the Weeks Act, a law enabling the federal government to purchase huge tracts of land that would be managed for large-scale logging under leases to big companies. Like the Adirondack forest reserve and park in New York, though, the national forest carved from the Minnesota iron range ran up against existing subsistence use on common lands—hunting, fishing, and trapping as well as running livestock, cultivating small garden plots, and logging for fuel wood. Most of the people who did this were Slovenian and Finnish miners supplementing their meager incomes, and their families were in especially dire straits after a drawn-out strike in 1907, when many leaders and other participants were blacklisted or simply laid off. The radical "red-flag outfit," a local newspaper contemptuously explained, "have taken off their best clothes and gone to the woods, in all probability to use some of the dynamite in blasting fish to fill their aching voids." Once the forest was created and new restrictions were in place, the same newspaper beat the drum against "pot hunters" among "foreign born residents," the "certain class of aliens" who worked the mines and railroads and hunted not for sport but simply for the meat, using various prohibited methods, violating set bag limits, and doing it even in the closed season.[41]

Not surprisingly, enforcement of fish and game laws in Superior National Forest was suffused with ethnic and class conflict. One area resident volunteered to serve as a game warden without pay to stop foreigners from poaching, particularly those who were fishing with dynamite at Burnside Lake, where he and a few other gentlemen sportsmen had erected lodges. The official game wardens were of the same mind as the sportsmen, clear about their foes and allies in the local community, and they felt emboldened to practice harsh treatment of conservation law violators. In April 1910, for example, warden Fred James shot and killed Andrew Metsapelto at Long Lake, alleging that he and several other Finns were net fishing. The incident brought a large, angry crowd to the jail where James was held, but the town's elite rallied to his defense and he was found not guilty when the case went to court. James was also known for gifting what he confiscated from fish and game law violators to town officials and business owners, once splitting a whole moose between the sheriff, police captain, justice of the peace, and several other friends. In this he was not unusual. Wardens and forest rangers were notorious for flouting fish and game laws themselves. "It's funny," one honest ranger wrote in a letter home, "everybody lives on wild meat here [at the ranger station] all the year round and they serve moosemeat to Forest supervisors and game wardens when they stop."[42]

Still, despite the unfairness of fish and game law enforcement as well as the hypocrisy of its initial advocates and those tasked with implementing it, conservation became somewhat less contentious in the decades following. Many foreign residents became naturalized citizens and began to play a greater role in the political and commercial life of the iron range towns, providing a check on ethnic prejudice. Miners and timber workers achieved more stable and adequate incomes through union activism as well, and with the creation of government-sponsored unemployment insurance they acquired other means of surviving economic slumps, making them less dependent on surreptitious use of the commons and more supportive of laws that managed fish and game for sport. In a change that was common throughout the upper Midwest during the 1930s and 1940s (discussed at greater length in the next chapter), iron range laborers of all sorts founded numerous local and county sportsmen's clubs, which they affiliated with state and national organizations like the National Wildlife Federation and (less often) the Izaak Walton League. The clubs maintained a working-class identity, however, one distinct from the gentlemanly character of other groups that more privileged sportsmen had established in the preceding era.[43]

"UNDER THE EXCLUSIVE CARE, CONTROL AND GOVERNMENT OF THE WAR DEPARTMENT"

Similar to Adirondack Park and Superior National Forest, the first officially designated national parks were plagued by profound social conflict as different races and classes struggled over competing uses of so-called wilderness, largely a choice between making a living there or preserving it for reflection and recreation. Many of the elites who promoted conservation were in the forefront of the preservation movement as well, seeking to protect wild places from the ravages of local people who were supposedly too uncivilized or backward to see that nature's greater intrinsic value. Wilderness was located in actual places—mountains, valleys, and canyons—but for its privileged advocates (notably white, wealthy men) it was overlaid or invested with a mix of very unscientific notions about the possibility of religious redemption, masculine regeneration, and national renewal. Even though they were clearly benefiting from industrial "progress," the preservationists were uneasy about certain aspects of the modern era, particularly what they themselves might be losing with the advent of manufacturing, the growth of cities, and the closing of the frontier. Some found solace outdoors, particularly in the midst of sublime scenery out West. The problem was that most of these areas were already occupied by human inhabitants, native people who had long made the places their home (and were otherwise mythologized as iconic "primitive ecologists" for their purportedly light touch on the land) as well as white, Hispanic, and black trappers, herders, and squatters who had arrived more recently. Since wilderness was by definition nature unchanged by human hands, these inhabitants had to go, and when they resisted, preservationists called on the power of the state.[44]

Yosemite Valley was first established as protected land by Congress in 1864, originally under the administration of the state of California, and then turned into a national park in 1890 after a fervent campaign led by the celebrated mystic John Muir. "Ax and plow, hogs and horses, have long been and are still busy in Yosemite's gardens and groves," he observed, and so he and others convinced the secretary of the interior to request U.S. troops to patrol the area. Captain A. E. Wood became the first acting superintendent there and led Troops I and K of the Fourth Cavalry into the park (just after chasing down Geronimo and his Apache band in Arizona and right before heading to the Philippines to put down Emilio Aguinaldo's popular insurrection for national independence). Other troops followed over the years, and the army was not fully withdrawn until 1914, once local residents were considered sufficiently pacified. Rangers with the newly established National Park Service began to patrol the area soon after (not coincidentally wearing uniforms that included a U.S. Army soft-brim "campaign" Stetson).[45]

For a time, some native people were allowed to stay at the park so that they could be put on display, regarded as part of the wilderness experience rather than antithetical to it. They resided in Indian Village, practiced various "native" crafts, and basically acted like generic Great Plains Indians, the highlight being the Indian Field Days festival every summer. To encourage native participation, historian Mark David Spence explains, park officials paid $1 to every man registered and $2.50 to every "squaw" appearing in "full Indian costume of buckskin dress, moccasin, and head decoration," all of which were foreign to Sierra Miwok culture. By the late 1920s, however, partly prompted by a report advising the restoration of park environs to their "pristine state," park officials began to question how well the "Yosemite," as they dubbed the local Indians, complemented their commitment to preservation, and when their Village was moved and shrunk and they lost employment in the park, native residents gradually moved away.[46]

At Yellowstone, established in 1872, threats from "bands of roaming savages" (actual Indians) as well as "white Indians" (equally lawless white settlers) provoked the likes of *Forest and Stream* editor George Bird Grinnell and Boone and Crockett Club founder Theodore Roosevelt to lobby for government intervention there too, while New York congressman Samuel Cox suggested putting the park "under the exclusive care, control and government of the War Department."[47] Subsequently, in 1886, Captain Moses Harris arrived with fifty cavalrymen from Fort Custer, Montana, and built Fort Yellowstone (near the Mammoth Hot Springs) in addition to scattered outposts and "snowshoe cabins" to support their patrols. "The intelligent rules of the Interior Department could only be carried out by military discipline," Charles Dudley Warren wrote in *Harper's* magazine, but the methods they used to clear the protected area and keep people out were sometimes questionably legal and not infrequently outright cruel. When hunting restrictions and campaigns against mountain lions, coyotes, and wolves caused an overabundance of elk, deer, and antelope, which competed with livestock for grazing lands, residents of nearby Gardiner had even more reason to run their animal herds in the park. The army put offenders in solitary confinement at Fort Yellowstone's guardhouse, sometimes for a month or more, on a diet of bread and water. In other cases, they separated the scofflaws from their livestock and marched them to the boundary farthest from the herd, which they scattered in the other direction, leaving the animals vulnerable to predators until the owner could return to round them up.[48]

Eventually, of course, national parks became something more like what their founders originally intended—vast tracts of protected, momentous scenery, free from despoiling human habitation—and within a few decades Yosemite, Yellowstone, the Grand Canyon, Glacier, and other grandly scenic places had become huge draws for workers and their families, eager to experience the outdoors on trips and vacations that helped affirm a "romantic" appreciation of nature. This was increasingly true as the country's economy changed and millions of native-born Americans as well as foreign-born immigrants exchanged rural farm work for urban industrial labor, making restorative escape ever more appealing. City life and factory work also gave those millions first-hand experience with pollution and other environmental problems, an experience that pushed a growing number to organize and protest. In the meantime, however, elites continued to disparage ordinary people's thinking and ways of living and consciously set themselves apart as the sole protectors of the nation's natural resources and wilderness. And that attitude played no small part in preparing the way for the *Silent Spring* origin story of environmentalism.

Taking nineteenth- and early-twentieth–century elites at their word, assuming that their self-proclaimed heroic efforts and version of events was unquestionably true, historians working in a number of fields cobbled together a fitting, complementary history. This was one that conveniently disregarded

several preceding decades of evident working-class environmental concern; largely ignored the ways in which the first
hunting and fishing laws, timber conservation policy, and
national park creation often privileged the interests of a wealthy
few over the mass of common people; and mostly identified conflict between those who were environmentally minded as a difference of opinion among elites themselves. With the past
framed in such a manner, it was an easy step for another generation of scholars, writers, and documentarians to then claim that
environmentalism emerged only after World War II, in response
to concerns about quality of life shared by middle-class suburban dwellers and inspired by Rachel Carson's moving exposé
about pesticides. Unfortunately, once the "songbirds and suburbs" interpretation was established as given, and *Silent Spring*
achieved a near-sacred text status, it became nearly impossible
to undo the error.

CHAPTER TWO

"Why Don't They Dump the Garbage on the Bully-Vards?"

Nearly a third of the way through *Silent Spring,* in a chapter titled "Needless Havoc," Rachel Carson cited a few moments in the "depressing record of destruction" that man had written "not only against the earth he inhabits but against the life that shares it with him." This included the slaughter of buffalo for their hides and the near-extermination of egrets for their plumage. Added to this was "a new kind of havoc," the killing of birds, mammals, and fishes by exposure to more recent, indiscriminate use of chemical insecticides. "Under the philosophy that now seems to guide our destinies," she lamented, "nothing must get in the way of the man with the spray gun.... The incidental victims of his crusade against insects count as nothing." Several pages into the chapter, Carson mentioned a specific example, a 1959 state program to control Japanese beetles in southeastern Michigan by dousing numerous Detroit suburbs from the air, "without notifying or gaining permission of individual landowners." According to the Michigan Audubon Society, which she quoted, the pesticide fell "like snow," collecting "in the spaces between shingles on roofs, in eaves-troughs, in the cracks in bark and twigs, the little white pellets of aldrin-and-clay, no bigger than a pin head, were lodged by the millions." This was, apparently, the real event that became *Silent Spring's* opening fable about chemical apocalypse, and like the spraying in the fable, the Detroit spraying had serious, unintended consequences. The pesticide pellets turned every puddle into a possible "death potion," the Audubon Society lamented, and within a few days the conservation organization began receiving numerous calls about dead and dying birds, followed by reports of sickened cats and dogs.[1]

Carson also recounted several other cases of aerial spraying gone wrong in a succeeding chapter, "Indiscriminately from the Skies," including the incident that inspired her to write *Silent Spring* in the first place. During the mid-1950s, the federal government's Department of Agriculture began a "chemical war" against the gypsy moth, using the pesticide DDT, and in 1957 the campaign came to the towns and suburbs of Nassau County, Long Island. In response, a group of residents led by the "world-famous ornithologist" Robert Cushman Murphy sought a court injunction to prevent the spraying, which was denied. Eventually the case went all the way to the Supreme Court. The Court's justices were not interested to hear it, however, with the exception of William O. Douglas, widely recognized in conservationist circles for his autobiography *Of Men and Mountains* and one of the admiring reviewers who later made an *"Uncle Tom's Cabin* of a book" comment about *Silent Spring.* He believed the lawsuit was a missed opportunity to hear the alarms raised by "many experts and responsible officials" about the perils of DDT. In the end, however, it accomplished as much. "The suit brought by the Long Island citizens at least served to focus attention on the growing trend to mass application of pesticides," Carson explained, "and on the power and inclination of the control agencies to disregard supposedly inviolate property rights of citizens." The aerial spraying continued, but protests increased, and within a few years the DDT program was "abruptly and drastically curtailed."[2]

Undoubtedly, it was passages like these, besides *Silent Spring*'s very title, that identified the book so strongly with songbirds and suburbs, and it was that association, as well as the way enthusiastic readers, prominent intellectuals, and crusading government officials talked about and responded to *Silent Spring*, that tied American environmentalism so strongly to the country's metropolitan outskirts and the particular concerns of the residents there. That linkage was certainly fixed in the minds of mainstream, contemporary environmental leaders and the agendas of their organizations, from the more established groups like the Sierra Club and National Audubon Society to the newer ones like the Environmental Defense Fund (EDF) and the Natural Resources Defense Council (NRDC). It was also unquestioned as a starting premise in the first accounts of the movement's origins and brief history. "Environmental values were based not on one's role as a producer of goods and services," Samuel Hays argued in *Beauty, Health, and Permanence*, published in 1987, "but on consumption, the quality of home and leisure." Those folks leaving cities for suburbs in ever more massive waves, he suggested, carrying their supposedly newfound values, became the core of a new environmental movement.[3] Even in more recent scholarly books and articles, this focus on suburbs and their residents has not budged much. People "living along the edges of many American cities after World War II" felt an acute "alienation" or "estrangement" from nature, historian Christopher Sellers explains in *Crabgrass Crucible*, which came out in 2012, one that "pivoted around the home rather than the workplace." That experience, he insists, had historic consequences, among them that "a new movement calling itself environmentalism arose."[4]

Yet while many residents of American suburbs did demonstrate measurable support for a range of environmental causes during the 1950s and 1960s, there was an insidious social dimension to their "environmental values" and participation in environmental campaigns, one underacknowledged by Carson, environmental leaders, and environmental historians. Many suburb dwellers had moved to the metropolitan outskirts to escape not only the filth and congestion of growing cities but also the African Americans, immigrants, and poor whites they blamed for urban ills. Once there, they went to great lengths to exclude others, depending on realtors and mortgage lenders to steer away unwanted prospective buyers, invoking restrictive housing covenants against them (prohibiting an owner from selling to someone who was not white), and employing petty harassment as well as mob violence against the few objectionable residents who somehow managed to move into a neighborhood. Those methods and the segregation they accomplished effectively restricted the environmental amenities of the widely touted bucolic subdivisions (the spacious yards, undeveloped meadows and woods, modern utilities and reliable sanitation services) to a select group. At the same time, the exclusion confined millions of people who were not white or middle-class to life in decaying cities or poverty-stricken rural areas, along with inordinate exposure to pollution, from smothering smokestack emissions and chipping lead paint to acid mine drainage and toxic agricultural pesticides.[5]

It was, in fact, among those who were most immediately suffering the ill effects of industrialization in urban areas—not those later worrying over songbirds in the suburbs—that the first stirrings of modern environmental protest happened. This social ferment coincided with the large-scale migration from countryside to city as well as the exchange of farm for factory labor that took place several decades before suburbanization was truly under way. Between 1870 and 1920, more than 26 million immigrants came to the United States, an increasing number of them peasants from southern and eastern Europe, and most of them ended their journey in cities. On the eve of World War I, a steady flow of African Americans also began to abandon the land they worked as sharecroppers and tenants throughout the South, to cast their lot in the urban North, and they were joined by a stream of native-born rural whites from both southern and northern states. As they settled in, both immigrants and migrants adopted an environmental awareness steeped in the labor they did and the hazards they met in their workplaces, the working-class tenement districts and neighborhoods where they lived, and the local and state parks, beaches, and forests where they sometimes spent their leisure time. Additionally, their understanding of environmental problems was infused with a sense of how class inequality, ethnic prejudice, and racial hatred determined or at least conditioned their daily experience and affected their fates, whether or not they could expect to enjoy good health or know natural beauty.

Not surprisingly, the early development of environmental awareness and activism was particularly evident not only in New England, where the country's industrial revolution got its start, but also in the rapidly growing cities of the Midwest, where steel mills, auto plants, rubber factories, and stockyards were transforming the region's economy and landscape by the late nineteenth century. In some places, campaigns for sanitation improvements came through "sewer socialism," mustering working people's support for variants of radical political ideas about the common good as well as middle-class voters' exasperation with the entrenched government corruption that hindered larger business interests. Typically, this meant taking city services away from private contractors, who mainly sought their own profit, and putting them under a form of municipal control dedicated to the general welfare, providing services to all residents (rather than a select few) and operating them more cheaply and efficiently. In other places, this kind of change happened by way of Progressive reform, anchored in the idea that a clean and healthy environment was essential to making reliable citizens (and the corollary that a dirty environment encouraged civic lethargy, vagrancy, and crime). Settlement house workers in particular, middle-class white and black women dedicated to raising up the residents of poorer city districts, drew on the notion of "municipal housekeeping," using that gendered justification to make a claim for women to assert a greater public role in leading local people to challenge faltering governments. Their contemptuous ideas about the aptitude and character of migrants and immigrants in their midst frequently interfered with the community organizing they were trying to do, yet settlement house advocacy and the clubs that settlements sponsored did contribute measurably toward helping neighborhood residents call attention to the need for more water and sewer lines, regular street cleaning, reliable garbage and ash collection, as well as inspections and fines to reduce pollution from smokestacks.

Radical social movements and social reform efforts also aided ordinary city dwellers who sought to escape the filth and noise of workplaces and neighborhoods by campaigning for local public parks, accessible lakeshore beaches, and state forest reserves.

Typically, these spaces were associated with certain racial and ethnic groups as well as trade unions and anarchist, socialist, and communist organizations, thus linking community identity and cohesion with leisurely excursions and retreats outdoors, and they saw steadily increased use during the 1920s and 1930s. Later, after millions of young unemployed men were put to work as part of New Deal–era conservation programs, planting trees, maintaining trails, and enhancing amenities, working people and their families flocked to national parks and forests in ever greater numbers too. What's more, many ordinary city dwellers created their own sportsmen's clubs, to support growing interests in recreational hunting and fishing, and those clubs soon embraced other environmental advocacy, including fighting for state-level water pollution control laws. Meanwhile, settlement houses, social service agencies, and scouting groups, as well as new industrial unions born out of Depression-era organizing, widened the opportunities for working-class children to attend summer camps, adding to the various formative influences shaping their modern environmental consciousness.

"COMMUNITY HEALTH IS EVERYBODY'S CONCERN"

Popular movements for sanitation improvements at the turn of the twentieth century were most successful in cities where workers joined with middle-class reform voters to elect socialist or other independent reform candidates to office. This kind of alliance often came together when political corruption was so out of hand that municipal governments barely functioned, accumulating waste of all kinds made streets and waterways deadly hazards, and residents were especially eager to rid the mayor's office and city council of patronage and graft by taking services out of private hands. In Toledo, Ohio, this happened with a radical challenge to long-established Democrats and Republicans initiated by Samuel "Golden Rule" Jones, mayor from 1897 to 1904, serving first as a Republican and then, when the party refused to nominate him again, as an unaffiliated independent. While he was not a member of the Socialist Party, he believed in Henry Lloyd's idea of a Cooperative Commonwealth, a social order built on each person realizing that their self-interest was bound up with the common good and working for the fulfillment of the basic needs of all. Jones recognized that inequality was inherent to capitalism and advocated its abolition, although he thought this could occur by harmonious change rather than class struggle. This change would be realized in large part through municipal ownership, substituting "cooperative" capital for "competitive" capital, turning city government into the primary agent for achieving social democracy, and awakening pride and a sense of solidarity in city residents.[6] Still, Jones also understood that there would be some resistance to the reasonable march toward social progress, including by those involved in providing city services under contract. "It is the contractor's business," he noted, "not to see how much he can get for doing the work and do it well, but first, to see how much he can get for doing it, and next, how very little he can pay the laborer and how poorly he can do the work in order to increase his profits."[7]

By the late nineteenth century, Toledo certainly needed radical change, including a new approach to sanitation. The city first began to use contractors to collect householders' garbage and ashes in the 1880s, supervised by the board of health, but there was much evidence that the work was not done regularly or well. Part of the problem was Toledo's sudden and rapid population growth, from 89,000 residents in 1889 to 120,000 in 1895. This rate of increase put heavy demands on collectors, and contractors never served anything close to all of the premises. In 1889, contractor Fred Hopp removed garbage from only 8,746 houses and businesses, and in the 1890s, when the city council decided to end the board of health's oversight role, service became still more irregular.[8] Even then, before the social reformers took charge, some city officials understood that the failure to provide universal service was dangerous to everyone, rich and poor alike. Citing a notorious set of buildings known as "Barnes' Block," health officer C. L. Van Pelt bemoaned the failure to collect the garbage there. "If any epidemic should come," he noted, "it would find all those conditions which would increase its virulence, and give it a foothold in our midst." His fears were compounded by certain opinions about the type of the people who lived on the block and the close quarters they shared. The buildings crowded together "vicious and destitute people," Van Pelt complained, "(blacks and whites) under one roof," and among the whites he singled out "Polanders," a segment of the population "to whom a threatened epidemic has no terrors."[9]

In his first "Message" to the city council in 1897, after winning 70 percent of the vote, Mayor Jones acknowledged that the large number of collection sites as well as the lack of uniform receptacles explained some of the deficiency in service, but he pledged that his administration would get to the actual root of the problem. Citing "the character and the enormous number of complaints," his newly appointed health officer, Dr. L. C. Grosh, insisted that "the trouble is the result of either negligence or non-compliance with the existing contract." City council members disagreed, however, and in 1901 the city was still collecting garbage under a contract, one that Jones had vetoed, and in his annual message that year he reiterated his opposition. Past expe-

rience, he explained, was all "the argument needed against further trifling with the city's comfort and health." Yet his position
was also linked to a broader conception of justice. "Let us take
care of our own garbage on the day labor plan," the mayor said,
"then we can be just to ourselves and, in some measure, just to
the men who do the work."[10]

Jones never did get to see his hopes realized, however,
because he died in office in 1904, and it was left to his heirs to
finish what his movement had started, which they did by taking
a more organized approach, establishing an actual Independent
Party. Their candidate for mayor, attorney Brand Whitlock,
won with ease in 1905, and he was reelected three times more, in
1907, 1909, and 1911, ensuring the perpetuation of an activist
municipal government. In fact, during Whitlock's second term,
he finally managed to get the board of public service to assume
control over garbage collection. Later, signifying the ideals
motivating the independent movement, and the motivation for
this particular achievement, the board of health introduced its
annual report for 1911 with the injunction, "Community Health
is everybody's concern!"[11]

Similarly, civic-minded socialists played a part in bringing
public control over basic sanitation services to Milwaukee, Wisconsin, although again only after many years of failed attempts
to use private contractors and repeated exposés of scandalous
corruption. Until 1875, as public health historian Judith Walzer
Leavitt explains, the city had no garbage collection at all and
residents cast their waste into the streets for hogs that roamed
about or for immigrant "swill children" who scoured piles for
things they might be able to eat or sell. Neither the hogs nor the
children took away all of the garbage, though, leaving "back-
yards and alleys ... reeking with filth, smelling to heaven."

Concerned about the potential for these unsanitary conditions to breed disease, Milwaukee's first health officer, Dr. James Johnson, lobbied the city's aldermen to take charge of waste collection. They approved a measure that allowed each ward to arrange separate contracts for the work, which only half of them did, the next year not even that many, and by 1878 none did. This finally prompted the council to accept a citywide contract, but that did not solve the problem either. The city received twenty-five to thirty complaints a day, citing all manner of negligence and double-dealing. Private collectors did not regularly pick up the garbage or refused to collect all of the waste because they only wanted refuse they could sell to farmers for pig food or fertilizer. It was almost as if nothing was being done at all. "Take a stroll a few blocks in almost any part of Milwaukee," one resident exclaimed, and you will find "heaps of dirt, broken pavements, breakneck crossings, and uninviting pools of filth." Meanwhile, growing concern among those living in the outlying districts where collectors dumped the garbage they did pick up provoked other complaints, and contractors began putting the waste in Lake Michigan, turning the shoreline and nearby waters into a mess of putrid flotsam and jetsam.[12]

Overlooking the persistent problems with collection but recognizing the need for an alternative disposal method, Milwaukee's city council began a decade-long search for a company that could at least reliably burn or render the garbage and keep it out of the lake. For a few years, the Forrestal Merz Company operated a rendering plant that consumed most of the waste, but the odor was unbearable. So, the plant was shut down and collectors resumed dumping garbage into the water. In 1891, a group of local businessmen organized the Wisconsin Rendering Company to build another plant outside the city, but amid political disagreements and accusations of payoffs, that effort foundered too. The next year, during a closed-door meeting with no written record, the Forrestal Merz Company and Wisconsin Rendering Company consolidated, and together they submitted yet another bid to build the new plant, which aldermen accepted even though it was much higher than the previous bid, raising more questions about impropriety. Suspiciously, ten Democrats who had previously opposed a Wisconsin Rendering Company contract supported the new combined venture, and Republican alderman F. C. Lorenz exposed two Democratic "rings" that would receive an additional $45,000 a year (above and beyond the contract amount) with the consolidation. Despite the evidence of graft, there was no significant shake-up in the 1892 local elections, although new rumors of corruption began to circulate, and within two years Republicans routed the Democrats, inheriting oversight of the new rendering plant once it was completed as well.[13]

Not surprisingly, the new plant was not an improvement on previous facilities, and health officer Dr. Walter Kempster was soon overwhelmed by citizen complaints. He received 471 in the single month of June 1894, citing failures of both regular collection and proper disposal, and this prompted him to make an investigation of his own. On the day Kempster surveyed the Merz plant property he personally witnessed forty-eight tramcar loads of garbage, dead animals, and offal being emptied into Lake Michigan at the foot of the facility, much of which washed back onto the beach. City engineer G. H. Benzenberg also took a look and agreed that the shoreline was "liberally supplied with garbage." This led the pair to begin a campaign for municipal control, an effort helped along by yet more revelations of rival investors as well as city officials receiving cash payments from the Wisconsin Rendering Company, in one case leading to formal charges against assemblyman and company stockholder Charles Polacheck. During the next election though, in 1898, the Democrats and Republicans were challenged by the recently formed Social Democrats, mostly German American trade unionists, socialists dedicated to the principle that government should serve the people, and both of the older parties came out in favor of a municipal plant. After the incumbent Republican administration was swept from office, the new city council moved quickly to take over collection, using city employees, as well as build a new cremator, which opened in 1902. Subsequently, complaints about garbage pickup dropped sharply, and corruption was no longer a part of disposal.[14]

Still, it seems, Democrats and Republicans could not give up completely on graft, and a flurry of new charges and indictments against them convinced middle-class business reformers and others to support the Social Democrats. As a result, in the 1910 elections socialists not only won a strong majority on the city council but also won the mayor's office, the city attorney and city treasurer posts, one-fourth of the school board, and two-thirds of the county delegation to the state legislature, besides sending Victor Berger to Congress. Following these victories, they selected University of Wisconsin economics professor (and socialist) John R. Commons to study Milwaukee's sanitation services and, on his recommendation, completed the shift to municipal control by consolidating collection and disposal under the single authority of the public works department. This was in addition to other changes meant to extend the role city government played in protecting the health and welfare of city residents, including distribution of diphtheria antitoxin to poor families, more effective food inspection, and milk vendor licensing. Like the reforms that socialists brought to Toledo and elsewhere, this gradual extension of public authority by Milwaukee radicals further contributed to establishing popular legitimacy for state and federal government over public health and environmental quality more generally.[15]

"NOT A LADY'S JOB"

Similar to other industrial cities in the upper Midwest, Chicago, too, saw dramatic growth during the nineteenth century, expanding from a swampy village of 30,000 before the Civil War to a city of half a million inhabitants by 1880 and a million within another decade, reaching over two million by 1910. This rate of increase severely taxed sanitation services well beyond their capacity, especially since city leaders were not particularly concerned with improving and expanding them. To aid mostly rural immigrants and migrants as they struggled to endure the poor living conditions they encountered, a few dedicated (but privileged) women began to establish settlement houses, challenging expectations about the role women could play in public to address various urban problems, including environmental ones. Among the most famous of the settlements was Hull House, founded in 1889 by Jane Addams and Ellen Gates Starr on the near West Side, or the Nineteenth Ward. "I gradually became convinced," Addams later recalled, "that it would be a good thing to rent a house in a part of the city where many primitive and actual needs are found, in which women who had been given over too exclusively to study might restore a balance of activity along traditional lines." And in fact, near West Side residents had plenty of needs, with tenement dwellers tightly squeezed into generally dilapidated quarters among astonishingly filthy streets. Making matters worse, the area was a mix of foreign-born working people, namely southern Italians, Greeks, Bohemians, Jews from various parts of Europe, and Irish, people who Addams believed showed "little initiative" and were "densely ignorant of civic duties," requiring missionaries of a sort to help them shed their "Old World" ways.[16]

In one of their first ventures to model virtuous civic consciousness, Hull House women organized a campaign to improve garbage collection, which was then done under a contract controlled by the local ward boss, Johnny Powers. After fruitlessly forwarding thousands of complaints to the health department for several years, in 1895 Addams put in a bid to remove the neighborhood's solid waste herself. To no one's surprise, the bid was thrown out, but Chicago's mayor decided to appoint the Hull House founder to the position of local garbage inspector, and she selected settlement worker Amanda Johnson to be her deputy. They made their rounds through the ward every morning in a horse and buggy, and their meticulous work made news throughout the country, with newspaper articles often suggesting that women were inherently superior to men for "municipal housekeeping," treating the larger city like it was a traditionally female private domestic space. Yet that was not everyone's opinion. As Addams remembered, many near West Side residents "remained quite certain the task of garbage inspection was not a lady's job."[17] To stop the campaign, and hinder the settlement women's claim on a greater public role, Johnny Powers convinced the city council to replace the inspectors with new, temporary appointments, after which the ward boss chose a trusted friend to fill the new post. Hull House leaders and their local allies responded by running their own candidate for alderman. Although he lost by a wide margin, following the defeat Addams met with the mayor and commissioner of public works about the inspection system's dismantlement, and the commissioner made Johnson garbage inspector for the entire city.[18]

In the wake of their campaign to address inadequate solid waste collection, the near West Side settlement residents turned their attention to the district's almost unbelievably faulty system for removing sewage waste, its deficiencies made vividly clear by a typhoid epidemic in 1902. Although the inhabitants made up only one thirty-sixth of Chicago's population, they experienced between one-sixth and one-seventh of all deaths during the epidemic. "Evidently," a Hull House report mused, "there must have been some local conditions which favored the spread of the infection." Upon further investigation, it became clear that the aging sewer piping in the ward was "most imperfect," causing privy vaults and water closets to back up and overflow into basements, yards, and streets, and in more than a few cases large tenements had no sewer connections at all.[19]

While settlement workers encountered an eagerness among ward dwellers to have something done about the problem, this was coupled with widespread belief that the law was on the side of negligent landlords and "fixed" inspectors protected by unaccountable politicians. In many cases when people made complaints, official health inspectors completed reports saying there was "no cause for complaint" or "nuisance abated," and when they did send violation notices property owners ignored them with impunity. In one tenement, owned by an ex-alderman, the main waste pipe for the building was broken for nearly half a year, during which time the basement was flooded with filth, while a clogged water closet on the second floor caused sewage to seep through the ceiling to the floor below. Occupants reported the condition to the health department numerous times, yet nothing was done and the department had no record of any complaints. The owner made repairs only after he was threatened with a lawsuit, and the work done was so shoddy that within a month the tenement's condition was as bad as before. "The law, official courtesy, and official supervision," the settlement women bemoaned, "are all exerted in favor of the owner of the real estate as against the tenant and against the third and most important interest, the public health."[20]

Fortunately, there was more success with efforts to improve sanitation in the Packingtown neighborhood, near the stockyards, primarily because the settlement house there, affiliated with the University of Chicago, did more to empower those living nearby, including women. That was due largely to the militant disposition of its founder, Mary McDowell. She had come to the city as a young girl, stayed for a while at Hull House, and developed profound concern for the plight of working people during the Pullman railroad strike in 1894, after which she took charge of her own newly established settlement, making it a center for community activism.[21]

When the packinghouse workers went on strike in the summer of 1904, McDowell played a critical role in arranging negotiations between Amalgamated Meat Cutters president Michael Donnelly and the packers' representative, J. Ogden Armour, solidifying her credibility with the Packingtown community and prompting socialist writer Upton Sinclair to stay at the University Settlement while he did research for his exposé *The Jungle.* At the time, as Sinclair graphically described in the book's opening pages, the area was plagued by the foulest air, scum-covered waterways, and scattered piles of rotting garbage, inhospitable living conditions that were compounded by the extremely dangerous and unhealthy working conditions in the slaughterhouses, rail yards, brickyards, steel mills, and other nearby factories. McDowell, who was later nicknamed "the garbage lady," gave full attention to these problems as well. The University Settlement very intentionally encouraged environmental awareness and remediation campaigns among local people by hosting several clubs, including the Neighborhood Guild, a group of men and women who focused mainly on the fumes and pools of filthy water produced by a glue factory; several Cleaner Clubs, composed of children who identified sanitation problems in their neighborhoods and logged them at city hall; and a Women's Club, which concentrated on street, alley, and vacant-lot cleanup.[22]

In one case, during 1913, Packingtown residents campaigned to close four clay pits on Damen Avenue used to dump garbage, one by the city, two by private carting companies, and one by meatpackers (which they set on fire so that it constantly smoldered), all owned by former alderman Thomas Carey, who had dug the pits to make clay bricks and then leased them when he was done. Early in the campaign, McDowell joined a group of mostly Polish and Lithuanian immigrant women who marched on city hall to complain to the health commissioner. "Why don't they dump the garbage on the bully-vards," one of the women rhetorically asked, "why do they bring it near our homes?" The commissioner had no answer and said his hands were tied for lack of alternatives, but not long after neighbors won a temporary injunction against more dumping and then worked out a compromise that allowed only dry garbage and required a cover layer of lime. Within a few months, "dirty, dripping garbage wagons" were regularly violating the compromise and local residents resumed their protests. In the fall, six hundred Packingtown dwellers visited Alderman Pretzel and Alderman Lipps at their homes, and the alderman went to visit the pits, calling them an "outrage," although for a while longer the city council continued to dither over the matter. By that point, McDowell had started to immerse herself in the technical literature on alternative methods of disposal, and after a visit to Europe to study these methods she began to make presentations about what she had learned, eventually convincing the city to shut down the dumps and build a small reduction plant. Just as importantly, the larger campaign and McDowell's central part in it challenged traditional notions about women's public roles, demonstrating that environmental activism was in fact "a lady's job."[23]

"THE DANGEROUS TRADES"

As an urban sanitation campaign evolved throughout the American Midwest as well as in other parts of the country, a related "industrial hygiene" campaign emerged to address workplace injury and disease. Many of the same people were involved in both, and efforts that initially focused on the dangers of the shop floor eventually created a foundation for understanding how industrial pollution affected the community beyond factory gates. One of the early industrial hygiene activists was University of Wisconsin professor and socialist John R. Commons, who had aided the Milwaukee Social Democrats as they consolidated "sewer socialism" in that city. Following a fire at the Triangle Shirtwaist Company building in New York City in 1911, which left nearly 150 garment workers dead, Commons assisted Wisconsin state legislator Robert LaFollette in passing one of the country's first workers' compensation laws, including measures to protect worker health and safety. He also helped found and lead the American Association for Labor Legislation

(AALL), which created a national commission on industrial hygiene, hosted several conferences on industrial disease, and initiated a study of phosphorus poisoning in the match industry. When inhaled, white phosphorus caused "phossy jaw," starting with swollen gums, progressing to abscess and rotting in the jawbone, and ending with organ failure and death. Led by John B. Andrews and Irene Osgood, the AALL study produced a damning report that led to federal legislation establishing a prohibitive tax on the compound and banning its import and export, thereby effectively eliminating its use by matchmakers.[24]

Another key figure in the evolving industrial hygiene movement was Alice Hamilton, a professor of pathology at the Women's Medical School of Northwestern University and a resident at Hull House. Like other settlement house reformers of the day, she dedicated her life to ministering to the needs of her poorer, often foreign-born neighbors, in her case by helping the "wops" and "hunkies" and others (as one employer described his workers to her) suffering unchecked abuse in the most "dangerous trades." Early on, she directed a study for the Commission on Occupational Diseases (in Illinois), beginning with the white lead, lead pipe, and paint industries, coordinating the work of twenty-three physicians, medical students, and social workers, in the hopes of eliminating occupational lead poisoning. Later, the study broadened its scope to investigate the dangers of arsenic, carbon monoxide, cyanide, and turpentine. After the final report was delivered to the governor, in 1912, Illinois passed workplace health and safety legislation as well, requiring various safety measures, monthly medical examinations for employees who handled lead and arsenic, and employer reports for all cases of illness (which the Department of Factory Inspection was empowered to use to investigate and prosecute violations). Subsequently, at the federal

Bureau of Labor, Hamilton led more studies on lead poisoning in the pottery, tile, and porcelain-enameled sanitary ware industries, investigated the manufacturing of storage batteries, and began probing into the dangers of the rubber industry. Then, in 1919, she was appointed assistant professor of industrial medicine at Harvard University, in the Division of Industrial Hygiene.[25]

Once the number of states with worker compensation laws reached a critical threshold (twenty-three states had passed laws by 1915), employers had a new incentive to address workplace hazards that might lead to compensation claims. To do that, they supported the work of medical and engineering experts, many of whom were on the Harvard faculty with Hamilton, and together they brought the science behind occupational health and safety to a new level. Relying much more heavily on controlled laboratory experiments, yet another investigation of lead poisoning established that lead was more toxic when inhaled than when swallowed (a common misconception). It also determined how lead was absorbed, stored, and eliminated from the body and developed an effective treatment for "lead colic." This and other work over the next two decades eventually spawned the more general field of environmental health. Wilhelm Hueper, for example, got his start studying workers' bladder cancers in Du Pont's dye works, and later, as head of the Environmental Cancer Section of the National Cancer Institute, he looked at the role other industrial chemicals played in rising cancer rates more generally (a source that Rachel Carson used and cited without acknowledging Hueper's background).[26] At midcentury, when a thermal inversion trapped a poisonous cloud over a zinc works in Donora, Pennsylvania, killing seventeen and causing thousands of respiratory cases, the United Steel Workers (who represented the workers at the plant but who also cared about the effects of the plant's pollution on the workers and their families who lived nearby) called on the U.S. Public Health Service to investigate. When their report proved inconclusive, the Steel Workers funded an environmental health study of its own, which played an important part in getting Congress to pass the first federal clean air legislation in 1955.[27]

"A PLACE TO DREAM"

From the late nineteenth to the early twentieth century, working people in industrial cities experienced an unequal share of environmental problems in their neighborhoods and at workplaces, encountering much of the immediate surroundings as a threat to their physical well-being. Like the New England mill girls a century before, however, they also knew "nature" as a place to encounter beauty, feel respite, and restore their health. Again, Chicago provides a good example. Close to home, city residents regularly visited numerous playgrounds, pastoral parks, lakeshore beaches, and commercial parks, and as affordable transportation brought the "recreational hinterland" near, they traveled to the Cook County forest preserves and various private resorts, including Camp Sokol, Illinois Turner Camp, Idlewild, Camp Pompeii, Camp Chi, Harcestwo Camp, and the Chicago Federation of Labor's Camp Valmar. Along with their own personal witness to Chicago's failures in municipal sanitation and industrial health and safety, these ventures to nature played a formative role in working people's developing environmental consciousness and, as Colin Fisher argues, helped different groups forge and maintain a community identity. While privileged, native-born whites tended to use rural and wild landscapes to imagine themselves as (exceptional) Americans,

Chicago's "rank and file" used both local and distant outdoor spaces to assert and affirm distinct ethnic, racial, and class identities. Many of the municipal parks, commercial gardens, and lakeshore beaches were associated with a particular group (and in some cases these groups violently protected their claim on those spaces), while the resorts hosted a narrowly defined set of patrons. Organized activities in each of these places were likewise anchored to specific aspects of the users' identity.[28]

Initially, as African Americans migrated to Chicago from the rural South, they were dispersed throughout the city and encountered little resistance when they sought access to outdoor amenities, often intermingling there with whites. By the 1890s, however, white racism began to harden, black residents were increasingly concentrated in racially delimited neighborhoods, and various places for recreation were soon closed to them or open only on segregated terms. Still, community leaders frequently encouraged working-class African Americans to escape the smoke and grime and roar of city life, if not in "the wild," then in local parks or at the lakeshore, which at least might "afford a breathing space, a place to dream," and they eagerly heeded the call.[29]

Increased black use of recreational space only heightened tensions, however, and with more migrants coming to Chicago at the onset of World War I, white attacks on blacks attempting to take their leisure became common. For two weeks during June 1918, for instance, "white hoodlums" roamed Washington Park and ambushed African American visitors they encountered, without regard to age or gender, chasing people down, beating some nearly unconscious, and throwing others into the lagoon. Typically, city officials, park directors, park police, and lifeguards were complicit in such violence, even sometimes aiding and abetting it, and the thugs acted with impunity. It was, then, hardly a surprise when a confrontation at the "white" Twenty-Ninth Street beach on a sweltering summer day in 1919 turned into a full-fledged, citywide race riot. After a group of African Americans attempted to use the beach, whites started to taunt them and throw rocks. Meanwhile, out near the end of a jetty, a raft with four black teenagers drifted into the "white" area, and a white man showered them with rocks too, causing one of the kids to fall off and drown. This event provoked a general melee on the shore that spread into adjacent neighborhoods. For the next four days white gangs attacked African Americans, but some black residents fought back too, and ultimately 38 people were left dead, 537 injured, and 1,000 homeless.[30]

In the wake of the riot, black Chicagoans continued to seek and find nature where they could, often describing their more distant outings with a combination of lyrical romantic musing and resilient race consciousness. One visitor to the West Michigan Resort described the place as Arcadia, "a forest of Arden bounded by a vast expanse of blue water" under a sky "rich with golden clouds and a streamer of sunlight," the "great trees" protecting him "from the worries of life." As the Associated Negro Press reported in 1925, many African Americans had discovered a love for "hunting, rowing, [and] hiking," a good thing since these activities were conducive "to better health conditions," and they added, "there is hope that thousands in the congested cities may more and more become interested in God's great outdoors." Many among the black elite found their escape at Idlewild, a resort in rural western Michigan. Scholar and activist W. E. B. Du Bois insisted that nothing compared to the lakeside retreat "for sheer physical beauty, for sheen of water and golden air, for nobleness of tree and shrub, for shining river and song of bird and low, moving whisper of sun, moon and star." Another part of its attraction, however, was the chance it gave "the sons and great-grandchildren of Ethiopia" to come together as a race.[31]

Poor black children in all-black Boy Scout and Girl Scout troops and YMCA and YWCA groups also made trips to forest preserves, lake dunes, and one or another rural camp, where they had their own chance to "swim in the warm, crystal lake water, fish, go canoeing and boating, make overnight hikes, go hunting, and [do] many other things which you cannot do in the city." In fact, back in Chicago, as the 1920s proceeded working-class black residents generally reasserted their claims to nearby beaches and parks as well, including the 372-acre Washington Park, which they began to call Booker T. Washington Park. There and elsewhere, park directors and staff held annual pageants that remembered aspects of African and African American history, using that shared past to instill a hardy race pride.[32]

In a similar fashion to the way blacks found respite and forged a sense of community outdoors, Chicago's anarchists, socialists, and communists also used urban parks and rural resorts to escape workplace drudgery and city life as well as build a radical labor movement. In the nineteenth century, the city harbored a strong eight-hour-day campaign, one that culminated in a massive strike on May 1, 1886—the first May Day—including a march to the lake shore where a crowd of ten thousand listened to speakers explain the "divine law" of eight hours for work, eight hours for sleep, and eight hours for recreation. The next week, at a rally in Haymarket Square, a bomb exploded and a fight ensued that left eight police officers and four rally participants dead. This set in motion a backlash, with hundreds of arrests, numerous warrantless searches of homes and offices, and the execution of four anarchists. Nevertheless, radicals persisted in their campaign for the eight-hour day, and they turned May

Day into an international workers holiday, which they annually celebrated in various public parks and commercial gardens. Over time, Chicago Federation of Labor (CFL) leaders such as John Fitzpatrick likewise encouraged worker militancy and solidarity by means of local park picnics and garden parties. When he ran for mayor in 1918, Fitzpatrick's platform included support for the eight-hour day, a pledge to address poor garbage collection service and excessive air pollution, and a plan to establish more urban parks and forest reserves on the urban fringe.[33]

During the 1920s, labor unions and radical organizations began to develop outdoor recreation programs too, the first of which was a summer camp sponsored by the Women's Trade Union League on the edge of the Palatine Forest Preserve, where "factory girls" might restore their health in a natural setting. Shortly after, the CFL purchased land for "Camp Valmar," a lakeside resort in Wisconsin where members enjoyed camping, swimming, boating, horseback riding, skiing, baseball, fishing, and duck hunting. The resort also served as a "melting pot," the labor federation promised, a beautiful natural place where workers could forget their differences and realize the overarching importance of banding together as a class. Similarly, the Young People's Socialist League operated eleven-acre Camp Yipsel, just north of the city, which the league's magazine described as "the biggest vehicle for better comradeship that we ever hit on." The Communist Pioneers had a camp as well, Lake Paddock, in Kenosha, Wisconsin, where young communists slept in an oak grove in tents named for communists heroes, ate together in Lenin Hall, and attended lessons on labor history, with other time carved out for hiking, swimming, and other sports.[34]

Later, during the 1930s, as a new worker militancy was born, radical neighborhood councils and unions affiliated with the

Congress of Industrial Organizations (CIO) continued to bring members together with park picnics, excursions to forest preserves, and camp outings. In one case, Polish Russell Square residents, who lived in the shadow of the South Works owned by the U.S. Steel Corporation, established Camp Lange on a wooded bluff overlooking Lake Walton. There the steelworkers' children could lose themselves in "the eternal green of nature" and forget "litter-strewn alleys, the booming noise of toiling mills, the blasting echo of slag dynamite and ever present pall of smoke from the open hearth and blast furnace." In another case, Polish, Lithuanian, Mexican, and African American Packingtown residents used CIO funding to send their kids to Camp Pottawatomie, on the Tippecanoe River, where play in nature served the double purpose of helping them bridge ethnic and racial differences and enhancing class consciousness.[35]

"NO FEAR OF THE GATHERING DARK"

Rural America served as the site for the development of urban industrial workers' environmental awareness in a different way in the 1930s when the Depression descended on the nation and millions of young, unemployed men were sent from the cities to the woods, deserts, and plains as part of a federal resource conservation jobs program. President Franklin Delano Roosevelt had created a model for the national program when he was still governor of New York, putting ten thousand unemployed to work converting abandoned farmland into public forests, and after this proved to be a success a handful of other states began forestry work-relief initiatives of their own. By the time Roosevelt entered the White House in 1933, the country's economy was in even worse shape, with nearly 40 percent of the nonagricultural labor force jobless, and he hurriedly moved relief and recovery legislation through Congress, including a law that established the Civilian Conservation Corps (CCC). Headed by Robert Fechner, leader of the International Association of Machinists and vice president of the American Federation of Labor, the CCC limited enrollment to unemployed, single men between the ages of eighteen and twenty-five whose families were already receiving public assistance. Recruits received $30 a month, but most of that had to go back home (which would help stabilize the economies where they came from) and they needed very little money where they were sent in any case. They slept in tents or barracks, ate in common mess halls, and only rarely went into town (if there was a town nearby). Mostly the men worked, planting trees, maintaining access roads and bridges, blazing trails, constructing picnic shelters and sanitary facilities, and terracing fields.[36]

Initially, many recruits were despondent when they arrived at a camp, missing the few comforts and familiarity of the places they left behind. Posted to the Ozarks in Arkansas, for example, Robert Ross could not help but feel deep repugnance for the natural world he confronted there. "Mountains surrounded me and hemmed me in," he recalled, "bushes with thorns on them, and the clinging vines that snarled and twisted around one's feet.... This was all so foreign to me, I hated it at once."[37] Yet most, including Ross, eventually adjusted and even grew attached to the landscape where they lived and labored, seeing how favorably it compared to bustling urban neighborhoods and streets. "Little did we realize," one young man wrote from his Pennsylvania camp in 1935, "that there was untold happiness awaiting us in this forest refuge, away from the artificial pleasures of the city."[38] Another recruit, E.D. Rennacker, expressed similar sentiments about his hillside camp in Fairfax, California. "The quiet hills and deep ravines," he mused, "revive my memory of scenes I had forgotten in the strife of civilization's noisy life." But sitting under the branches of a huge oak tree, "years older by many seasons than me," Rennacker found solace in "Nature" and comfort despite a general feeling of despair, and he had "no fear of the gathering dark." Gerald J. McIntosh, also at an Ozarks camp like Ross, even went so far as to question the tradition of cutting trees for urban dwellers to buy at Christmas, turning something wondrous into a cheap commodity. He contrasted the loud cry of the "huckster" selling trees for a mere fifty cents with "the stately trees back in the forest green, that I had left the day before—May God preserve the scene!"[39]

Besides experiencing changes in their own attitudes, the Civilian Conservation Corps recruits greatly affected the thinking of the people in the communities where they worked and those well beyond, demonstrating the merits of forest- and soil-management methods and spreading knowledge about basic principles of ecology to the wider general public. Those who had firsthand experience with CCC projects could not deny their real impact. By the time the program was done in 1943 participants had planted two billion trees, effectively reforesting whole parts of the United States, and they slowed erosion on 40 million acres of farmland, greatly helping farmers facing imminent failure and raising yields by leaps and bounds. But Americans in every region of the country, Neil Maher explains, "read about Corps camps in local newspapers and national magazines, and even watched full-length feature films portraying CCC conservation projects." This exposure had significant, measurable results. Although Roosevelt's critics had originally objected to the program as wayward socialism (or alternatively, the germ of fascism), within a few years it had achieved the same legitimacy among the general public as public libraries, city water systems, and the postal service. In 1936, 82 percent of Americans surveyed wanted the corps to continue its work, and three years later that support was even higher, cutting across party lines and regional divides. At one and the same time, the CCC provided basic relief, moved the economy closer to recovery, and overcame the last vestiges of resistance to government conservation prevalent among common people at the end of the nineteenth century.[40]

The only reason the Civilian Conservation Corps was shut down was to free up labor and resources for war production and allow some young men to go into the military, yet even then it continued to shape ordinary Americans' thinking, values, and habits. This included their use of state and national parks and forests, where the CCC had done so much to improve amenities and make them accessible. Visitation to national parks alone increased from less than 3.5 million in 1933 to 16 million in 1938 and to 21 million in 1941, then more than doubling again to 56 million by 1955.[41] But people were just as inclined to escape to nature locally. In Massachusetts, at Harold Parker State Forest, within easy driving distance of Lawrence, Lowell, and Boston, there had been two Civilian Conservation Corps camps and they completely transformed the area, once a logged out "waste land." The recruits planted fifty thousand white and red pines, made ten miles of footpaths, built and stocked several ponds, laid out a dozen campgrounds (each equipped with rubbish barrels, picnic tables, and sanitary facilities), and constructed sixty-seven stone fireplaces.[42] "Every weekend," the *Lawrence Eagle Tribune* reported in 1937, "hundreds of cars from the Hub [in Boston] carry merry families to the woodland playground."[43]

Ironically, the advancing "democratization" of parks and forests provoked concern and opposition among some of the leading lights in the conservation and preservation movements, who (they themselves claimed) had been trying for so long to instill an appreciation of nature in common people. Taking stock of the expansion of popular leisure time, more widespread car ownership, and rapid road building, people like Aldo Leopold, Robert Sterling Yard, Benton McKaye, and Robert Marshall began advocating to keep inaccessible places inaccessible. By mid-decade, some of these figures were so worried they began a campaign to enact federal legislation that would carve out a vast "wilderness system," defined at least in part by restrictions that would keep designated areas undeveloped and roadless. Moved forward by the Wilderness Society, headed by Howard Zahniser, this campaign culminated in passage of the Wilderness Act of 1964, initially protecting more than 9 million acres of federal land.

"THE COMMON MAN OF MODERATE MEANS"

One of the other indications that ordinary Americans' attitudes about state and federal conservation policy were shifting from indifference and resistance to accommodation and support was the dramatic growth in working-class sportsmen's clubs. These clubs, first established in the 1920s and 1930s at the county and regional levels, were usually affiliated with state organizations as well as national groups like the National Wildlife Federation (the Izaak Walton League was more typically associated with elite sportsmen). Their primary purpose was to advocate for fish and game management that would enhance members' outdoor recreation experiences, including habitat protection, hatchery and stocking programs, hunting and fishing season restrictions, and licensing. But these practical concerns were bound up with the desire to use nature as an antidote to the trials of modern industrial life as well. "Of course, your first thought is to be that of downing game," one bow-hunting club journal explained, yet "equally as important is the God-given opportunity to get away from teeming cities and the rush of everyday living and plant your feet on the good soil of a backwoods trail."[44] Additionally, without actually calling themselves "environmentalists," the working-class sportsmen began to pay close attention to the threat posed by municipal and industrial pollution, and they were among the most important advocates for environmental regulatory legislation before midcentury.

In Michigan, where the auto industry dominated the economy, various factors came together to make forests, fields, streams, and lakes popular destinations not just for "prominent citizens of business and of industry" but for blue-collar autoworkers too.[45] On the one hand, mass production of cars was regimented, dull work, seemingly removed from nature, aspects especially evident to recently arrived rural migrants used to self-directed farm labor outdoors. On the other hand, mass production innovations greatly lowered the prices of cars, turning what were once playthings for the wealthy into affordable transportation even for the people who made them, providing the means for escape from industrial cities back to the hinterlands. The Model T that cost $1,200 in 1909 cost only $300 in 1928, an amount within reach of most factory hands. From the turn of the century to the start of World War II, workers also won more "free time" as a result of corporate "welfare capitalism" schemes, union contracts, and federal wages and hours laws, whittling the average workweek down from sixty hours to the standard forty hours and allowing for the expansion of paid vacation benefits.

And finally, there was an increasing number of places for Michigan's working-class sportsmen to go. By the mid-1940s in the downstate area alone there were thirty-four public hunting grounds and thirteen recreation areas (most of which were open to hunting), plus the Allegan State Forest, a total of 117,000 acres of land.[46]

The true watershed of popularity for working-class recreational hunting and fishing, though, came after World War II, when each year more than 1.5 million Michigan residents purchased licenses and took to the fields, forests, streams, and lakes with rifle, bow, rod, or traps. In 1948, for example, nearly a quarter of a million Wayne County sportsmen (and some sportswomen), many of them line workers at River Rouge, Highland Park, Hamtramck, or one of Detroit's other car plants, purchased hunting and fishing licenses. That same year, Genesee County residents, most of them employees at General Motors in Flint, purchased fifty thousand deer and small game licenses, and Oakland County residents, including workers at the GM plant in Pontiac, purchased fifty-nine thousand fishing licenses.[47] Testament to this broad interest, the ranks of local sportsmen's clubs grew tremendously, sustaining membership lists in the thousands, an even larger monthly newsletter circulation, and regular lively meetings. The local clubs' growth also expanded the Michigan United Conservation Clubs (MUCC), headed by Vic Beresford, who was secretary of the Wayne County Sportsmen's Club based in River Rouge as well. Within ten years of its founding in the 1930s, the MUCC had 250 affiliates, easily rivaling the older Michigan Izaak Walton League and giving it considerable influence with state political leaders.[48]

Not surprisingly, the sportsmen's clubs' evolving concerns evidenced their class perspective in a variety of ways. Columns in newsletters advised readers to support proposed legislation that would end bans on Sunday hunting, for instance, a policy that still prevailed across the state. Only a little more than half of the downstate hunting areas (the ones closest to many workers) were open on Sunday, editors of the *Macomb County Sportsman* complained, even though it was "the only day when many hunters can go afield." Another article, in the *Genesee Sportsman*, took aim at the threat posed by wealthy individuals and private clubs who could afford to buy land and bar public access and so deny "the common man of moderate means" a place to hunt and fish.[49]

When they acted on growing apprehension about pollution, club members demonstrated a certain kind of working-class political engagement and social consciousness too. Hunting and fishing clubs will have outlived their usefulness, the *Kent League Sportsman* put it, "if they [are] organized merely for the stocking, feeding and protection of a single species, without regard to their obligations to the public, without respect to nature and science, without regard to human rights." In line with that perspective, Genesee County sportsmen set up a Water Pollution Committee to address municipal sewage waste and industrial discharge in the Flint River, and a number of groups started a petition campaign in response to a fish kill in the Kalamazoo River caused by Union Steel's repeated release of cyanide into the water. The Kalamazoo poisoning was, in fact, one of the incidents that prompted sportsmen to demand a state regulatory law, and in 1949 governor-elect G. Mennen Williams addressed Michigan United Conservation Club directors to say that the legislation was among his first priorities. Soon after, with much lobbying on the part of local clubs and the MUCC, and despite the opposition of what they called "industrial lobbyists," a bill passed and Williams signed it into law.[50]

"INSIGHT INTO DEMOCRATIC LIVING"

In much the same way that sport hunting and fishing evolved from elite leisure activities into broadly popular recreation, during the first half of the twentieth century summer camps went from being exclusive domains of the high-born to inclusive cultural melting pots. First established in the late 1800s, the original camps were meant to allow boys from privileged families to temporarily escape the city for the body- and character-building experiences "wild" nature might afford them. There they would live "live a free, outdoor life" while "having at all times the sympathetic companionship of young men of refinement."[51] By the 1920s, however, there were thousands more summer camps in the United States, most of them in the Northeast and Midwest, and many were open to working-class youth, including both boys and girls from various ethnic and racial backgrounds. This was due in large part to the rise and spread of scouting, with the founding of the Woodcraft Indians in 1901 and the Sons of Daniel Boone in 1905, which combined to become the Boy Scouts of America several years later, and with the creation of the Camp Fire Girls in 1911 and the Girl Scouts in 1912, organizations that operated their own inexpensive outdoor retreats. Moreover, they were complemented by an increasing number of camps run by settlement houses (like Hull House and the University Settlement in Chicago), urban charitable organizations (like the YMCA and YWCA), and industrial labor unions (notably those affiliated with the Congress of Industrial Organizations), each with their own varied emphasis.

By the late 1940s, several of the numerous summer camp programs available to Michigan and Ohio youth were run by the
United Auto Workers (UAW), which represented employees at
Ford, Chevrolet, and General Motors and their suppliers, the
very same factory hands who were expanding the ranks of local
sportsmen's clubs. The UAW's first camp, established in 1947,
was the Franklin Delano Roosevelt–CIO Labor Center, eight
miles north of Port Huron, Michigan, on the Lake Huron shore,
open to boys and girls ages eight to fourteen whose parents were
members of the union. As one of the promotional brochures
proudly announced, "Now UAW-CIO Members Can Afford to
Send Their Children to Camp Too." For a nominal cost, autoworkers' kids could sample a range of activities, including hiking,
swimming, boating, softball, volleyball, nature study, and camp-
fires, amid 200 acres of woods and beach, allowing them adequate opportunity and space "to learn to live and play together
the CIO way." And when the Labor Center began to fill beyond
capacity, the UAW International office partnered with Toledo
(Ohio) UAW Local 12 to open another camp on Sand Lake, just
west of Detroit, also providing ready access to outdoor recreation that would give children "leadership training in self-gov-
ernment" and "insight into democratic living."[52]

Throughout the rest of the 1950s and into the 1960s, the two
UAW camps hosted thousands of union members' children, and
they continued to blend appreciation for nature with liberal-
minded socialization. Roaming the woods, fields, marshes, and
beaches at Port Huron and Sand Lake was meant to be part of a
traditional romantic escape to nature "out there," but both struc-
tured and unstructured activities were also very much intended
to prepare campers for civically engaged lives "back home." "It is
the 'togetherness' of nature and wholesome group living," a Port

Huron camp brochure explained in 1962, "that make a camp vacation a never-to-be-forgotten experience."[53] That same year, in fact, hundreds of college students used the camp to hold the founding meeting of Students for a Democratic Society, which many point to as the start of a radical New Left, and they announced their agenda with the "Port Huron Statement." "We seek the establishment of a democracy of individual participation," the statement declared, "governed by two central aims: that the individual share in those social decisions determining the quality and direction of his life" and "that society be organized to encourage independence in men and provide the media for their common participation."[54] More or less, this is exactly the spirit and thinking the union had wanted to see flourish at the camp, and although the students later demonstrated significant differences of opinion with the liberal UAW leadership, they shared many of the same ideals and concerns, including awareness of ever-worsening air and water pollution. Together, during that decade and into the next, both youth activists and union militants played important roles in helping to build a modern environmental movement. But they also never lost sight of the ways in which the environment was interwoven with other common interests, including the battle for industrial democracy, the fight to end poverty, and the struggle for racial equality.

CHAPTER THREE

"Massive Mobilization for a Great Citizen Crusade"

When Rachel Carson first set out to write an exposé about the hazards of synthetic pesticides she went through a couple of different working titles, including "Control of Nature" and "Man against Nature."[1] These phrases evoked another well-known book about humankind's rapacious use of natural resources, George Perkins Marsh's *Man and Nature; or, Physical Geography as Modified by Human Action,* published almost a hundred years earlier, in 1864, also to great acclaim and influence. Marsh's book was one of the key sources that New York legislators cited in pushing for the creation of Adirondack State Park, which significantly limited human activities in the woods there, making little distinction between big logging companies or elite leisure sportsmen and homesteaders practicing a long-held "moral ecology" for their subsistence. Like her nineteenth-century counterpart, Carson too had a tendency to indict an abstract "man" for various environmental problems, balking at placing more specific blame on those few who had the wealth and power to wreak the greatest harm and ignoring how social divisions and inequality condemned particular groups of people to experience a disproportionate share of the consequences (as well as the sharpest bite of new restrictive conservation and environmental regulations). "In the age when man has forgotten his origins and is blind even to his most essential needs of survival," she declared at one point, "water along with other resources has become the victim of his indifference."[2] What's more, her book's final title, *Silent Spring,* seemed to suggest that the culprit was so obviously "man" that he did not even need to be named, while likewise insisting that the most noteworthy impact of "man's war against nature" was poisoning songbirds.

To be sure, there were a few points in *Silent Spring* where discussion centered on a more specific explanation for why something so dangerous as pesticides was so prevalent and unquestioned. The modern era was one "dominated by industry," Carson insisted at the end of her second chapter, "in which the right to make a dollar at whatever cost is seldom challenged." The finished manuscript also included four chapters (of seventeen) that highlighted the harm pesticides did to people, rather than the single chapter (of twelve) the author had originally planned, and there were short case histories scattered throughout. Additionally, the year after *Silent Spring* was published, in April 1963, CBS aired a companion television program, "The Silent Spring of Rachel Carson," and the opening shots were shockingly clear about the danger pesticides posed to birds and people alike, although concern was tellingly focused on those living in the suburbs. The program began with Carson on her porch at her seaside home in Maine and then brought in her voice-over, reading a line about chemicals being the sinister partners of radiation, nonselective weapons that kill everything, a warning paired with footage of a crop-duster flying over tract houses, an out-of-place machine (not unlike a war plane) sent to an otherwise pleasant neighborhood on an insidious errand. Later, in June of that same year, Carson testified before the Senate committee chaired by Abraham Ribicoff and made two particular recommendations. One was strict control of aerial spraying (which would rein in the kind of pesticide application that opened the television program) and the other was eventual elimination of persistent pesticides (which would protect those like the tract-house residents who consumed foods grown with a growing array of agricultural chemicals).[3]

Oddly, however, field and orchard hands, the people who probably suffered the most direct, frequent, and prolonged exposures to pesticides, did not make much of an appearance in *Silent Spring*. There were a few mentions of exposure from dusting and spraying on farms in the "Elixirs of Death" chapter, including a reference to nearly a dozen men sickened by parathion while picking oranges in Riverside, California, a case Carson used as an example of how unsafe even less persistent organophosphates were. "The danger to all workers applying the organic phosphorous insecticides in fields, orchards, and vineyards is so extreme," she explained, "that some states using these chemicals have established laboratories where physicians may obtain aid in diagnosis and treatment." But the next and only other full-sentence acknowledgment of the risks farmworkers faced was not until chapter 12, "The Human Price," halfway through the book, and that statement was overly general. "The sudden illness or death of farmers, spraymen, pilots, and others exposed to appreciable quantities of pesticides are tragic," Carson wrote, "and should not occur."[4] Despite this clear expression of empathy, *Silent Spring* failed to investigate any further the extent of the problem or why such tragedy did occur, how it was that growers could subject their employees to routine chemical poisoning with impunity.

In Riverside and other parts of southern California, most of the farmworkers who did the spraying, tending, and picking were Mexican and Filipino migrants, poorly paid and badly housed and fearful of demanding safe working conditions. Federal and state laws establishing standards for wages and hours, providing unemployment insurance, and guaranteeing the right to form a union and bargain collectively with an employer did not apply to agricultural workers. In any case, many of the Mexican field and orchard hands were undocumented, vulnerable to arrest and deportation if they asked for proper field reentry times, safety equipment, medical monitoring, or hospital care. The problem was not only the manufacture of dangerous pesticides and their use—which Carson described in her book at length—but also the power wielded by corporate farmers to make field and orchard hands do their bidding without complaint or resistance—which Carson skirted. Class and race simply did not figure in her explanation of "man's war against nature," and so she missed the ways in which that battle was inextricably linked to "man's war against man." By the 1950s, in fact, when the California Department of Public Health began to track illness linked to the use of pesticides and herbicides, agriculture had a higher rate of occupational disease than any other sector of the state's economy, and most cases were coming from Los Angeles, Fresno, Kern, Tulare, and other southern counties known for the substantial migrant population working huge "open air factories."

Fortunately, there were community activists willing to help southern California field and orchard hands to organize, and unlike Rachel Carson, they were actually quite aware of the ways ethnic prejudice, economic exploitation, and environmental injustice were interlayered. The organizing campaign started in 1962, when César Chávez and Dolores Huerta moved to the San Joaquin Valley, where they had earlier established a chapter of the Community Service Organization, a grassroots initiative dedicated to Chicano civil rights. Building on that effort, they established the National Farm Workers Association, which eventually merged with the mostly Filipino Agricultural Workers Organizing Committee to form the United Farm Workers Organizing Committee. By the mid-1960s the union was on strike against table-grape growers and began to focus increased attention on the dangers of pesticides, in part because it was such a serious threat to orchard hands and in part to bring consumers to their side. Volunteer nurse Marion Moses set up a health and safety commission to investigate workers' exposure, while lawyer Ralph Abascal examined application records, lab analyses, and lawsuits, after which the union called for a boycott. As the struggle went on, the union made numerous appeals that linked their fight to a larger environmental movement as well. "More and more people are aware of the poisons in the air, water, and food and throughout the environment, and are frustrated from feeling they can't do anything to stop the onsurging [*sic*] wave of contamination," one 1969 handbill declared, but "boycotting grapes is one of the very few ways the American consumer can act with proven effectiveness AGAINST pollution."[5] True to this argument, when the United Farm Workers won their first contracts with growers, they gained significant health and safety protections, including provisions prohibiting the use of DDT, aldrin, dieldrin, and endrin and restricting the use of other pesticides, well beyond anything required by existing state or federal law at the time, and a benefit, as the union pointed out, "to workers and consumers alike."[6]

Although the farmworkers' organizing campaign is important in its own right, it is also an instructive example of the varied contributions that organized labor and other community activists made to environmental activism in the years after World War II more generally. Some unions, like the United Auto Workers (UAW), supported workers' outdoor recreation and concern about environmental problems as a matter of their broader Cold War liberalism. Other unions, like the United Farm Workers (UFW), were solidly grounded in 1960s-era radicalism and always made a very explicit point to connect environmental and social justice. Additionally, similar to the fight waged by orchard and field hands, there were countless environmental campaigns rooted in community activism that focused on poverty and pollution tied to ethnic prejudice and racial inequality. From efforts to deal with numerous environmental hazards in Cleveland during the 1960s to the fight against a hazardous-waste landfill in Warren County, North Carolina, in the early 1980s, this kind of environmentalism was marked by sophisticated analysis of what was wrong, innovative militant tactics to make things right, and specific local goals that were always connected to a broader reordering of American society as a whole. It was only by willful disinterest that so-called mainstream environmental leaders, environmental historians, journalists, and others failed to see how it fit prominently (rather than marginally) in the American environmental movement.

"STOP THOSE WHO POLLUTE FOR PROFIT"

Just as working-class sportsmen (and sportswomen) founded local hunting and fishing clubs to support their particular outdoor recreational interests, factory workers (many of the same people, in fact) helped organize labor unions to protect their distinct economic interests on the shop floor. During the 1920s and 1930s, in Michigan and other midwestern states, much of that organizing was focused on the auto industry. As a result of the effort, including factory occupations and pitched battles with police and National Guard troops, by the start of World War II all three of the major auto manufacturers and their numerous suppliers had officially recognized the United Auto Workers as the sole bargaining agent for their hundreds of thousands of employees. Over the next several decades, under the leadership of Walter Reuther, the UAW won contracts that improved workers' wages and hours and simultaneously promoted a social democratic vision that went well beyond those basic concerns. Central to the expansive vision was support for education and recreation programs that nurtured rank-and-file members' social and environmental consciousness as well as advocacy by union local leaders and International officers for municipal, state, and national pollution controls. While it might seem counterintuitive considering the industry the UAW was associated with, by the 1950s the autoworkers' union was playing the leading role among organized labor in addressing environmental problems while at the same making vital contributions to the larger modern environmental movement.

Within the union's Recreation Department, established in 1939, the guiding philosophy emphasized the need for workers to be thoughtful about how they used their leisure time in order to make up for the alienating drudgery they experienced on assembly lines. Everyone needed to relax after a hard day's work, director Olga Madar acknowledged, but what factory hands did during their time off was also critical for feeding the "mental and spiritual cravings which must be satisfied if we are to become complete and happy individuals." The main thing was that recreation activities not be motivated by "a dollars and cents reward." Planting a row of beans in the garden could save the family money, and yet the primary satisfaction came from "turning the soil over on your spade, and thinking ahead a few days to the time when the young plants will poke their noses through the soil." Likewise, hunting might be "better if you bring home a deer," but that was not necessary to make a trip "fun."[7]

Most importantly, Madar believed, a union member's leisure determined "much of the difference between being a good and useful satisfied citizen in our democracy," and her department led the UAW in lobbying for more public outdoor recreational resources where autoworkers and their families could spend a worthwhile afternoon, weekend, or extended vacation.[8] This was often in collaboration with local sportsmen's clubs as well as the Michigan United Conservation Clubs and National Wildlife Federation (NWF). As Walter Reuther prepared to give the keynote address at the 1963 NWF conference, for example, Madar helped him by suggesting remarks that not only identified recreation "as a public service to benefit all people, regardless of income level," but also opposed any legislation that established admission fees for federal and state parks. Two years later, the Recreation Department made a list of pending bills to watch during the imminent legislative session, including one that would require state anglers to pay a license fee, likewise contrary to the idea that "recreation is a legitimate social welfare function and, as such, should be financed through the general fund and further insure to all citizens free access to public recreation areas."[9]

Madar always viewed concern with pollution as part of her department's work, but she and the UAW's other leadership increased their level of engagement with the issue over time, and by the 1950s, when the union had close to 1.5 million members, it rivaled traditional preservation and conservation organizations in state and national influence. Demonstrating this influence, in 1965 the UAW hosted an unprecedented conference on clean water in Detroit, drawing more than a thousand union, sportsman, and environmental delegates from both Canada and the United States. "I am hopeful that this conference here today can be the beginning of a massive mobilization of great citizen crusade," Walter Reuther exclaimed to the audience in his opening speech, "not only in terms of fighting for clean water, but for cleaning up the atmosphere, and the highways, and the junkyards and the slums and all the other things that we need to do to create a total living environment worthy of free men." This was meant to put environmentalism at the service of Cold War liberalism, melding campaigns to address pollution with efforts to make a "Great Society," the wide-ranging agenda dedicated to ending poverty and challenging racial inequality that President Johnson had announced a year before at the University of Michigan. Yet Reuther understood the effort would not be easy, likely hindered by both recalcitrant government and irresponsible industry, and it would not happen simply by the decrees of leaders alone. The particular marching orders he gave everyone at the clean water conference included a call for community organizing. Neighbors had to join together at the state level as well as nationwide "to begin to come to grips with the problems of neglect, with the problems of indifference which are destroying, not only our natural resources, but which are corrupting and corroding the very environmental atmosphere that we breath and live in each day of our lives."[10]

The UAW officially committed to the growing environmental movement in 1967 by creating a new Department of Conservation

and Resource Development, appointing Madar to serve as director and giving her a seat on the International executive board.
That same year, Madar made a statement before a Senate subcommittee in support of tightening federal standards for auto
emissions, which the auto industry opposed. The union favored
environmental regulatory controls even if they had an adverse
impact on jobs, she said, because autoworkers had "to breathe the
same air and drink and bathe in the same water" as everyone
else.[11] The new Department of Conservation also supported local
organizing, such as the Down River Anti-Pollution League
(DAPL), an ambitious project started in 1969 and encompassing
several working-class neighborhoods in the Detroit area that were
particularly affected by area industry. In the fall, the union
approved funding for two DAPL interns, who under Madar's
guidance surveyed (union and nonunion) residents, built a steer-
ing a committee, arranged initial meetings, and staged pickets at
water commission meetings. As part of this effort, for the first
Earth Day in 1970 Lincoln Park resident Joyce Vermillion led a
group of league women joined by women from Pollution Probe of
Ontario in a protest against the Great Lakes Steel blast furnaces
on an island in the Detroit River.[12] In addition, that summer, a
group of self-described "UAW wives," with support from Madar
and her assistant, Charleen Knight, gathered to form another
organization, United Active Women, including a "Womenpower"
committee to handle mobilization and recruitment. They focused
on water quality improvement, lobbying the city council, and
leading tours of industrial pollution sites, and they did it with the
women's liberation movement's characteristic sense of humor. "Be
the first in your neighborhood," they wrote in one monthly newsletter, announcing the next site tour, "to breathe Down River's
famous hydrocarbons, sulphur dioxide, and carbon monoxide."[13]

The United Auto Workers also purposefully held its twenty-second annual convention that same spring, to coincide with Earth Day week, and prominently displayed on the main stage was a backdrop banner reading, "Enact—Environmental Bill of Rights ... The Right to Fresh Air, Clean Water, and the Enjoyment of a Healthy, Attractive Living Environment."[14] Surely Walter Reuther had something to do with that, but unfortunately his death in the Black Lake plane crash just days afterward meant that he did not get to see how his leadership on environmental issues came to fruition during the following decade. Despite the tragedy, the UAW went ahead with a planned environmental conference at the new retreat center later that year, an event attended by a range of labor leaders, community activists, and student radicals, meeting to develop a common agenda that focused on "urban and industrial pollution." They institutionalized this alliance in 1971 by organizing the Urban Environment Conference, which included the United Auto Workers, the United Steel Workers, and the Oil, Chemical, and Atomic Workers as well as the Sierra Club and National Welfare Rights Organization. Meanwhile, Conservation Department director Olga Madar made repeated trips to Washington, D.C., to testify in support of the Clean Air and Water Pollution Control Acts and subsequent bills to improve their reach and enforcement.[15] She also allied the UAW with the new urban activism building on the election of the first black mayors in various major northern cities, activism that advanced environmentalism as a social movement concerned with racial disparity and corporate greed. One pamphlet, "Pollution is Not a 'White Thing,'" included a quote from Madar alongside another from Gary, Indiana, mayor Richard Hatcher, the second African American elected to a large city's mayorship, after Carl

Stokes in Cleveland. "The chief victims of pollution are the urban poor, Blacks and workers who cannot escape their environment," Madar said, and "unless we join together now to stop those who pollute for profit, our cities will soon become ugly cesspools of poisonous pollutants."[16]

"A MONUMENT TO MAN'S NEGLECT AND FAILURES"

Raised in Cleveland public housing by a single mother, Carl Stokes overcame childhood poverty and became mayor of the lakeside industrial city in 1968, serving two two-year terms. When he came into office Cleveland was suffering significant urban decay, extensive air and water pollution, festering racial disparity, and ceaseless white flight. Stokes had at least some understanding of how all these problems were connected, however, and his administration attempted to craft solutions with that in mind. Yet, as David and Richard Stradling explain, this was not an easy task. In the early part of June 1969, for example, the mayor spent a night with his family at home while police outside fired tear gas at a large group of angry white residents, enraged after a young black man stabbed a young white man to death following an altercation provoked by African American encroachment on historically all white neighborhoods. Later that week, Stokes attended a cornerstone ceremony at the Central National Bank's new downtown tower and announced a massive ten-year building and rehabilitation effort for Cleveland. The city was "a monument to man's ingenuity and enterprise, the rich repository of great commercial, cultural and educational achievements," he declared, but it was also "a monument to man's neglect and failures in the areas of deteriorated housing, air and water pollution, race relations, inadequate health care, high unemployment rates, inadequate mass transportation, high crime rates and insufficient attention to the problems of our senior citizens." The next week, the Cuyahoga River caught on fire, something that had happened nearly a dozen times before since the late nineteenth century and an event that made Cleveland the reference point for the environmental crisis plaguing American cities. Stokes led the press on a "pollution tour" the following day, to bear witness to the many pollution sources at the southern end of the city's industrial flats, including the Harshaw Chemical Company, where production waste turned the Cuyahoga various colors, as well as a defective sewer interceptor, which had already poured 1.4 billion gallons of raw waste into the river.[17]

Part of what sustained citywide support for the mayor's broadly cast urban reform agenda was historical precedent, something that he was certainly aware of and purposefully invoked. The month after he attended the Central Bank cornerstone ceremony, Stokes participated in a public birthday celebration for former mayor Tom L. Johnson, a contemporary and ally of Toledo's socialist mayors Samuel Milton Jones and Brand Whitlock, and he took the opportunity to draw parallels between past and present administrations. Standing in front of Johnson's statue, Stokes quoted him at length. "Good sanitary conditions, public parks, pure water, playgrounds for children and well paved streets are the best kinds of investments," he declared, "while the absence of them entails not only heavy pecuniary loss, but operates to the moral and physical deterioration of the city's inhabitants."[18]

The mayor's efforts also drew support because they were in line with what many Cleveland residents (and other Americans), whether black or white, well off or poor, understood the

environmental movement to be about, casually blending social
and environmental concerns. "Keep on fighting for fair housing
in the Lee Sevillle area and everywhere," African American
Willie L. Morrow wrote to Stokes during that fretful summer,
"keep on fighting for gun control laws, keep on fighting for air
pollution control, but most of all keep on fighting for a fair and
better government for the citizens of all races of Cleveland and
this great nation of ours."[19] Similarly, white youngsters from the
city's surrounding suburbs revealed an acute awareness of the
fact that environmentalism raised larger social questions. After
conducting several "studies" on their city's pollution problem,
Westlake High School student Andrea Rady wrote, one example that stood out to her was the coal-fired Municipal Light
plant, which she described as "both an eyesore and a health hazard to anyone coming within 1 mile of it." Sixteen-year-old Debbie Mohoric, from Maple Heights, was even more bold: "People
or profit?" she rhetorically asked. "Do you want to conquer pollution or do you want pollution to conquer us?"[20]

Sometimes overwhelmed by the sheer weight of the social,
economic, and environmental problems he faced, and challenged
by shifting national priorities as President Nixon rolled back his
predecessor's war on poverty and vigilant effort to end racial inequality, Mayor Stokes did not always act and speak consistently
or tactically about environmental issues. In particular, when he
invited environmental activists to city hall to start "Environment
Crisis Week," leading up to the first Earth Day in 1970, he used
that moment to stand down from highlighting environmental
problems. "I am fearful that the priorities on air and water pollution may be at the expense of what the priorities of the country
ought to be," he announced, "proper housing, adequate food and
clothing." Several activists called him on this (knowing that he

had usually been an important environmental advocate), and he conceded their points, but a month later the *New York Times* also chided him for the comment. "It is sad to see so fine a mayor as Carl B. Stokes of Cleveland succumbing to the notion that the fight against pollution can only be waged at the expense of the poor," the editors wrote, since "these two vital sets of demands are interwoven aspects of the same environmental problem."[21]

In fact, just after the Environment Week opening, the mayor called on "all members of our community to endorse the April 15th march against the war in Vietnam," citing the war as a drain on the attention and resources needed for "grave domestic needs" like "lack of housing, pollution of our air and water, and inflation." At the end of April, Stokes also traveled to Washington, D.C., to support a water pollution control bill introduced by Maine senator Edmund Muskie, and there he voiced the source of his earlier frustration. "Frankly, on Earth Day, just a few days ago," he testified, "I was not particularly impressed with the Congressmen and Senators and mayors and legislators and members of the administration who fanned out across the nation giving speeches about the terrible threat to the continuity and longevity of this nation, because there is no question in my mind but that those same Congressmen, those same Senators and legislators and very often the mayors will be reluctant to try to face what it would cost to do something about that which they were speaking so pointedly and so brilliantly on the various podiums throughout the nation."[22]

By the fall of 1971 Mayor Stokes was exhausted by the different forces arrayed against his efforts. Despite some notable successes— including more than four thousand new public housing units, a large federal grant to create "vest pocket" parks on abandoned and unkempt lots, an enhanced air pollution code, and a $100 million clean water bond—he took stock of what remained to be done and decided not to continue his political career. "In 1967, it still seemed that the cities could be turned around," he explained, yet "three years later the economic tide had turned and we were headed for even more problems than before." Suburban growth had left the central city with a high concentration of poor residents as well as an ever-diminishing tax base, and after a failed attempt to raise the income tax to make up some of the difference, the municipal government stopped hiring and started drastically cutting department budgets. Among the hardest hit was the Recreation Department, which lost millions of dollars needed to actually maintain its existing and recently created parks and playgrounds. The impact of other cuts was also devastating, but there were few alternatives. "You cannot look to the people in the suburbs," Stokes explained, "because that is why they are out there," and you cannot look to the state "because the legislature is controlled by a suburban-rural coalition." Only the federal government could "reach to suburbs, make them part of a health or transportation or air-and-water pollution control system, make them help support the city."[23]

"BLACK SURVIVAL IN OUR POLLUTED CITIES"

Although having an empathetic mayor advocate for a city's poorest residents could effectively draw attention to serious problems, the frustration Carl Stokes experienced is emblematic of how little that could accomplish on its own. In some places across the United States African Americans left behind in deteriorating cities by fleeing middle-class whites also attempted to respond to systemic neglect with community activism. Often this centered on a campaign to abate lead poisoning among children confined to densely populated urban ghettos, partly because the problem was so endemic and had such serious implications and partly because it could actually be measured with medical tests.

Lead paint use had begun to increase everywhere in the 1930s and 1940s, but (white) absentee landlords in inner-city areas during the decades following did little to maintain the places they rented, while housing inspectors failed to force them to make needed repairs, and peeling paint became a significant health hazard. By midcentury, millions of children (who were particularly vulnerable) were suffering from the acute or chronic effects of lead exposure, including cognitive debilities, behavior disorders, seizures, comas, and even death. What's more, industry spokespeople were resistant to shouldering any responsibility for the crisis, blinded by greed and racism. "Aside from the kids who are poisoned," Lead Industries Association's director of health and safety Manfred Bowditch wrote to one of his colleagues in the mid-1950s, "it's a serious problem from the viewpoint of adverse publicity." He acknowledged the greater frequency of lead poisoning in the "slums" and insisted that the solution was to educate parents. "But most of the cases are Negro and Puerto Rican families," Bowditch explained, "and how does one tackle that job?" Those parents, he said, were "relatively ineducable."[24]

In St. Louis, according to historian Robert Gioielli, the first public concerns about lead originated with veteran civil rights activists. Many of those folks were working with War on Poverty agencies and programs, like the Model Cities program, established in 1967 to aid social welfare and physical reconstruction projects in targeted urban neighborhoods, and they helped found and sustain various community groups and organizations with that in mind. One of the more important organizations they created in the predominantly black northside was the

Yeatman Community Health Center (YCHC), which in 1969, with a grant from the Kellogg Foundation, established the Environmental Field Program. African American scientist Wilbur L. Thomas, Jr., served as the center's first director, receiving invaluable assistance from radical fellow scientist Barry Commoner, who headed an interdisciplinary research laboratory at nearby Washington University. Both men believed that civil rights, poverty, and the environment were linked issues, and in February 1970, in a speech to students at Southern Illinois University Edwardsville, later published as "Black Survival in Our Polluted Cities," Thomas boldly explained the connections. Because of racist economic and political structures, he said, inner-city blacks were forced to bear a "double burden" or "double dose" of environmental threats, those that affected almost everyone as well as those more likely to plague black communities specifically, lead poisoning being a notable example.[25]

After nearly a year of community pressure, and just a month after Thomas gave his "Black Survival" speech, the St. Louis city council passed a law to address lead poisoning, but it was fundamentally flawed. It split enforcement responsibility between the health department and housing division, the one handling paint chip testing and blood sample analysis and the other doing home inspections and court appeals, causing much confusion and long delays. Consequently, activists continued to demand effective regulatory oversight, and lead abatement figured prominently in the first Earth Day celebration a few weeks later. To organize local participation for that, Thomas joined with social worker Freddie Mae Brown to found and advise the St. Louis Metropolitan Black Survival Committee, which wrote and performed a play highlighting environmental issues as well as other inner-city concerns. "It seems to me that our efforts to better black conditions have been too narrow to help all the people," one character mused. "I think we must begin to fight all the problems that make for our slum environment." Perhaps responding to media reports about Mayor Stokes's dismissal of air and water pollution as a high priority, another character insisted that pollution was "much too important to leave it for whites to solve for us." And in the play's final speech, a powerful challenge to the notion of environmentalism as a movement about songbirds and suburbs, the whole cast declared that the health problems associated with the city environment, including lead poisoning, rat bites, and respiratory ailments, did not just happen to occur in the ghetto; they happened *because* of the ghetto.[26]

During the months following Earth Day, with an expansive environmental justice perspective guiding them, northside residents stepped up their lead campaign and began to adopt confrontational tactics. The Yeatman Community Health Center established another group specifically for this purpose, the People's Coalition against Lead Poisoning (PCALP). In early August, PCALP supported Carrie McCain, her daughter, and other activists when they went on a rent strike and staged a sit-in at the realty company that managed the apartments where they lived. McCain's granddaughter, Dorothy Nason, had been treated twice in six months for lead poisoning, but landlord Charles Liebert had failed to address the problems in his apartments. When Liebert responded by evicting the family, a Legal Aid lawyer took him to court, successfully arguing that McCain had a right to withhold her rent until the landlord made necessary repairs. Meanwhile, activists continued to coordinate testing and treatment for thousands of other children, pushed the city to revise the lead paint law and provide better enforcement, and dedicated more efforts to providing safe, affordable housing. They also began to look beyond St. Louis and collaborate with others outside the city. This was greatly facilitated by the first National Black Political Convention in Gary, Indiana, in 1972, attended by thousands of black community leaders. The convention's final platform included environmental concerns as a major plank, demanding "a living environment before profits" and calling for an urban Environmental Protection Agency. Shortly after, in fact, the EPA (created by President Nixon in 1970) issued a report titled "Our Urban Environment and Our Most Endangered People," noting that white, middle-class flight to the suburbs was sapping cities of resources, speeding their decay, and leaving those too poor to move to suffer the consequences.[27]

"PREPARED TO PROTECT OUR LAND BY WHATEVER MEANS ARE NECESSARY"

At the same time that many common people were confronting the environmental consequences of urban decay, often leavened by a sharp awareness of the disproportionate impact caused by persistent racial inequality, other ordinary Americans were confronting the environmental ravages of industrial capitalism in the countryside, similarly informed by an understanding of the role that racial prejudice and cultural stereotypes played there. In southern Appalachia, where age-old mountains harbored vast timber, coal, and other natural resource reserves, hill and hollow dwellers long dismissed as ignorant, inbred, fatalistic "hillbillies" mustered militant opposition to surface coal mining. Surface extraction, or strip mining, had become increasingly common in the years during and after World War II, primarily because it required far fewer miners and so lowered labor costs. Besides threatening the jobs of deep miners and offering little in the way of economic diversification, strip mining caused significant environmental harm too, including deforestation, acid mine drainage, and soil erosion. Sometimes, following heavy rains (not unusual in the region), massive landslides destroyed farms, orchards, barns, and even homes, and in a few cases they buried people alive. Yet in the wake of the devastation the typically "small" operators who dominated this part of the coal industry did little or nothing to restore or reclaim the landscape.[28]

For various reasons, strip mining's environmental effects and social impact were particularly bad in eastern Kentucky. Hillsides there were comparatively steep and state regulatory laws (first passed in 1954) were especially weak and poorly enforced. In addition, the state supreme court had ruled (also in the mid-1950s) that "broadform" deeds, which separated mineral and surface rights, allowed operators to disturb land and buildings above ground to get at coal seams below without obtaining permission from owners or compensating them. Consequently, as surface extraction expanded in the area and coal operators willfully disregarded permitting and reclamation requirements, eastern Kentucky mountain dwellers began to speak out and organize. In the fall of 1960, Letcher County resident Raymond Rash sent petitions to the governor with more than a thousand signatures demanding strip mining's end. Surface extraction "destroys the surface for agricultural purposes," he wrote in a cover letter, "throws immense amounts of loose earth into the streams, causes mud to be carried down onto our gardens and crop lands, and into our wells, and destroys the natural beauty which God has so lavishly placed in our region." Even the local Chamber of Commerce supported the petitions, convinced, as the secretary-treasurer noted, that surface mining would have "calamitous results on the economy of the counties involved and will do much long-range harm to the economy of the entire state." Taking stock of this and other sentiment against stripping, in 1963 legislators amended the original regulatory law, but the new provisions mainly addressed problems faced by farmers in western Kentucky, where rolling farmland posed fewer challenges for controls and restoration. Meanwhile, problems in the mountains only worsened.[29]

By the summer of 1965, tensions in eastern Kentucky had reached a breaking point, and when Richard Kelley and Bill Sturgill sent their bulldozers to start clearing land owned by Dan Gibson in Knott County, they provoked a pivotal confrontation. After he spied the machinery, Gibson went to the top of a nearby ridge with a rifle and warned the men below against coming any farther. Sturgill agreed they would not continue and the elderly coffin maker then gave himself up to police officers, but after a boisterous group of gun-toting neighbors surrounded the Hindman jail, all charges were dropped and he was let go. A few weeks later, at least eighty people met and pledged their willingness to continue to resort to sit-ins, lie-ins, and armed standoffs to keep strippers from their land. Following that meeting, an even larger gathering of folks formed the Appalachian Group to Save the Land and People (AGSLP), and one of their first official actions was a fifty-car motorcade to call on the governor, by which time they had three thousand names on abolition petitions circulated in both Knott and Perry counties.[30]

AGSLP activists also continued to directly assist landowners in their efforts to stop coal operators from encroaching on their property, most famously when sixty-one-year-old Ollie "Widow" Combs called on them to help protect her homestead in Honey Gap that November. When bulldozers came to her land, Combs called Dan Gibson, and he went over with four other men to find many more already there, every one of them armed, and they scared the strippers away. Several days later the mining crew returned and Combs and her sons were alone, so they sat in front of the bulldozers, the police arrested them, and they ate their Thanksgiving dinner in jail, which made a perfect picture on the front page of the state's main newspaper, the *Courier Journal.* The governor responded by counseling citizens to obey the law but noted "that history has sometimes shown that unyielding insistence upon the enforcement of legal rights by the rich and powerful against the humble people of a community is not always the quickest course of action."[31]

Within a few years, organizers had established AGSLP chapters in almost all of the eastern Kentucky counties, still focusing on lobbying legislators and supporting lawsuits but increasingly relying on nonviolent direct action (like blocking bulldozers and haul roads) and defending homesteads with guns. "We must point out to you that a bulldozer moves much faster than the courts and legislatures," members declared to coal industry representatives at a 1967 reclamation symposium, "so while we wait for action by the state, we are prepared to protect our land by whatever means are necessary." The Appalachian Group was opposed to violence, they insisted, "but we cannot help noticing that the only language the strip-mine operators understand is the language of bullets."[32] Frustrated with the meager results of their efforts, some activists began to employ industrial sabotage as well. Working under the cover of night, they dynamited millions of dollars' worth of machinery at several surface mines, doing it so efficiently and thoroughly that everyone assumed the culprits were deep miners familiar with explosives.[33]

By the early 1970s, in fact, surface mining opponents had completely given up on affecting change through state courts and state government. "We are here to consider and evaluate our position under the power of industrial corruption," Letcher County native Warren Wright declared at a 1971 "People's Hearing on Strip Mining" that included more than two hundred participants from Kentucky, West Virginia, Tennessee, and Ohio. Because judges and legislators were too crooked and heartless, he insisted, "we must attempt to bypass them."[34] Subsequently, while they continued to use extralegal methods in the local hills and hollows, Kentucky activists shifted their attention to the need for federal intervention and, joining with folks from other states who were waging their own campaigns, they started to work on a legislative ban at the national level. To do this, in the fall of 1971 various groups from throughout the mountain region, including Save Our Kentucky, Citizens to Abolish Strip Mining, Stop Ohio Stripping, and the Wise County Environmental Council, established the Appalachia Coalition. Throughout the rest of the decade, the coalition played the central role in pushing for passage of an abolition bill.

"FREEING THE BEACHES"

Inspired by the example of so many other social justice campaigns during the 1960s and 1970s, in both cities and rural areas, activists also brought confrontational protest tactics to the seashore as part of a turbulent "open beaches" movement. Postwar development at places like Connecticut's "Gold Coast," stretching along the western edge of Long Island, had created hundreds of exclusive beach communities that closed off miles of shoreline to everyone except their wealthy white residents.

They accomplished this, as Andrew Kahrl explains in a history of the Connecticut fight, by limiting parking availability or banning street parking altogether, charging excessive fees to non-resident visitors, and erecting physical barriers, including fences and seawalls that disturbed the local ecology and made the landscape more susceptible to storm damage. In a bid to keep state and federal governments from forcing them to open their beaches, some Gold Coast communities decided to forgo public funding for environmental management as well, declaring that they could do that on their own.[35]

Yet inland residents challenged the bold attempts to turn the shore into a private dominion, insisting that the beaches were a public resource for all to enjoy and, just as importantly, one that necessarily needed coordinated state and federal regulatory oversight. To these critics, exclusion was legally dubious, socially objectionable, and environmentally perilous. "One would have to live in a vacuum," one report explained, "not to suspect that many beach restrictions are based in part on racial motivation, intermingled with the idea of building a wall between city and suburb." Likewise, the Connecticut Department of Environmental Protection (DEP) noted, the "parochialism and narrow interests" that sustained resistance to managing the coastline as a whole, particularly opposition to public wastewater treatment facilities, posed grave threats to ever-shrinking wetlands and shellfish beds.[36]

One of the things that allowed privileged Gold Coast residents to close the shore to others was the state assembly's willingness to authorize private "beach associations," which increased in number from a dozen in 1920 to nearly five times that by 1960. These associations had the power to levy taxes, regulate land use, and restrict public access, and they were the primary institutional means for members to maintain a community's "character." Additionally, coastal towns guarded their traditional zoning powers and jurisdictional autonomy, zealously wielding them to determine who could and could not afford to live there, further extending and preserving the region's "sand curtain." Nearly one-third of the 30,000 acres in Greenwich, for example, was zoned to require lots of no fewer than four acres, and in other cases towns prohibited multifamily and mobile homes outright.[37]

Meanwhile, noncoastal dwellers faced increasingly meager options for summer recreation, despite state and federal efforts to expand public open space. On weekends and holidays the Connecticut DEP turned away an average of five thousand visitors at Hammonassett Beach, the state's largest and most centrally located, and even families who did make it through the gates encountered scattered trash and filthy water. One visitor claimed that it was "physically impossible to put a blanket down without lying on debris washed up with the tides." And families without the means to drive to the shore faced even worse conditions on polluted waterfronts. Children swimming at beaches near Norwalk, Bridgeport, New Haven, and New London risked "gastric disturbances" and "non-paralyzing" viral infections, but public health officials hesitated to close the waters because they feared local slum dwellers would riot.[38]

For some observers and lawmakers, Kahrl notes, the apparently critical state of affairs at beaches in places like Connecticut demanded government intervention, and in 1969 they rallied behind a federal Open Beaches Act. Proposed by Texas congressman Robert C. Eckhardt, who had led the push for legislation in his home state a decade before, the law would have established "free and unrestricted right to use" beaches, prohibit "fences, barriers, and other restraints on the use of the beaches by the public," as well as empower the Department of the Interior and Justice Department to pursue enforcement. It also would have provided state acquisition of land for easements to ensure public access, limited local and state powers to rezone the shore for private development, and prevented property owners from erecting obstructions across a beach to exclude the public. Taken together, the separate sections were intended to protect remaining coastal wetlands and aid open access, both seemingly compelling reasons for passing the bill. "We are becoming a landlocked people," Texas senator Ralph Yarborough told his fellow lawmakers, "fenced away from our own beautiful shores, unable to exercise the ancient right to enjoy our precious beaches." Yet despite winning many supporters in both the House and Senate, a coordinated assault on the proposed legislation by coastal homeowners and real estate developers killed it in committee.[39]

Lacking relief from the federal government, in the early 1970s some Connecticut residents shut out of Gold Coast beaches began to rely on direct action to challenge the privileged elite's land claim. Central to the campaign was a social activist from Hartford, Edward T. "Ned" Coll, who in 1964 founded a group called the Revitalization Corps to address various basic needs of the state's inner-city children, organizing clothing and food drives as well as educational and recreational programs. He insisted on taking a broad view of urban social problems, however, linking them to white America's disconnect from and indifference to the poor. "Violence in the streets," Coll declared in a speech, "starts with the yawn in the suburbs." During the summer of 1971 corps volunteers gathered dozens of poor black children from Hartford and drove them to exclusive beach towns, spending the afternoons playing in the water while Coll went door to door asking locals to welcome a child into their home for the weekend. Mostly they met a cordial reception, but in late August, on a trip to Old Lyme, residents glared and shouted at them, mothers rushed their children off the beach, food stand vendors refused to serve black customers, and police threatened to arrest Coll, all of which served to give him an epiphany. The original point of the trips, he said, was having a good time, not "freeing the beaches," yet after the hostile encounter he became more adamant about drawing public attention to the racism and bigotry behind the resistance.[40]

In the years that followed, Coll staged many more similar protests in other coastal towns, hoping to get city kids on the beach or, at least, to subject access restrictions to public scrutiny, often against unrelenting opposition. In 1973, for example, in Madison, where the beaches were designated for town residents only, the health director insisted that corps children have a physical exam before visiting, the Recreation Commission cited "insufficient information" to deny them guest passes (for the hotel they checked into), and the zoning board prohibited the hotel from issuing guest permits altogether. This prompted Coll and his fellow activists to spend that summer and the next hounding residents at church services, town meetings, and the private beach club, including a stunt where they rowed boats around the club's stone piers and staked out space below the hide tide line for the day.[41]

Rather than eroding Gold Coast racism and snobbery, it seems, corps protests only hardened white, wealthy residents' determination. In Old Lyme, the activists' local headquarters was vandalized and eventually burned down, and in Madison, volunteer Anne Loiseau was brutally attacked by two unknown assailants, who slashed her face with a broken bottle. During the mid-1970s towns also passed more restrictive beach access laws while tightening existing ones. Greenwich, for example, which was already the most exclusive town in the state, barred nonresidents from walking or jogging along the beach, stiffened penalties for trespassers (anyone found above the high tide line), required nonresident visitors to petition the director of city parks and post a $250 bond, and added a guest fee.[42]

Civil liberties groups challenged the accumulating restrictions, filing more than 150 lawsuits between 1970 and 1985, citing the use of federal and state tax revenues to maintain beaches and other coastal features as an argument against barring nonresidents. State and federal lawmakers passed legislation to more explicitly tie government funding to open access as well. But this simply prompted wealthy communities to make an extra effort to forgo public money and refuse both state and federal coastal management, protection, and preservation, to their great expense and to the detriment of effective planning and oversight. "Let's be cautious that we are not trapped into using federal money in any way, shape or form to help pay off debt for purchases of our beaches or for their operation or maintenance," Madison selectwoman Vera Dallas advised, "which would jeopardize restricting their use to residents only."[43]

"THE NEGATIVE EFFECTS OF CHEMICAL CONTAMINATION"

At the same time that poor black urban activists were struggling for open beaches in Connecticut, residents in Love Canal, a suburban neighborhood located between Niagara Falls and Buffalo, New York, were discovering and responding to a deadly toxic-waste landfill in their midst, and both race and class factored significantly there. Although often characterized as an unprecedented prelude to the birth of an "environmental justice" movement, what happened at Love Canal was only one part of an already long history in community-based campaigns that fused demands for social and environmental change and employed confrontational tactics. Until recently the story that historians, environmentalists, and others told about residents' battle with public officials featured an oddly stripped down cast of participants and an attenuated chronicle of events. Elizabeth D. Blum recovers a much fuller sense of the story, however, setting the critical efforts of local housewives and mothers alongside the equally significant but largely forgotten involvement of white working-class union men (the husbands and fathers of the women who organized) as well as poor black women living in public housing (at nearby Griffon Manor). In doing that, Blum shows the full range of complicated interests involved. Mothers' worries about their children's health were central, she acknowledges, but in addition workers were apprehensive about multiple exposures to toxic chemicals at work and at home and the possibility of escaping the neighborhood despite plummeting home prices. At the same time, public housing residents were frustrated with their marginalization by home owners, media, and political leaders and agonized about being able to move their families anywhere safer without government assistance.

The problem at Love Canal began in the 1940s, when the Hooker Chemical Company obtained the right to dump waste into excavated holes from an earlier abandoned canal project, one that gave the neighborhood its name. The company eventually purchased the property from the city and, over the course of a decade, filled it with more than 21,000 tons of caustics, alkalis, fatty acids, and chlorinated hydrocarbons from the manufacture of dyes, perfumes, rubber solvents, and synthetic resins. Even then the dangers were evident. One longtime resident, Aileen Voorhes, whose home was adjacent to the canal area, remembered how waste drums would routinely break and catch on fire, and her daughter, Karen Schroeder, recalled helping workers burned by chemicals that spilled onto their clothes and skin. The men would run screaming into the yard, Schroeder said, and her mother would spray them down with the garden house before an ambulance arrived.[44]

Despite the obvious risks of exposure to the toxic waste, in 1953, when the dumping was complete, Hooker Chemical covered the area with dirt and sold the land to the Niagara Falls School Board for $1, whereupon officials oversaw the construction of an elementary school on the site, which was finished in 1955. By the mid-1970s, as the buried chemical drums deteriorated and especially heavy rains and snows saturated the ground, oily residue began seeping into basements and puddling on the surface. When *Niagara Gazette* reporter Michael Brown investigated and drew a link to health problems in the area, the city hired a consulting firm to look into the matter further. The firm recommended a cleanup project that would cost half a million dollars, however, at which the city balked. This led state environmental agencies as well as the federal Environmental Protection Agency to get involved, and it eventually prompted local residents to organize.[45]

One of the first people in the community to act was Lois Gibbs, whose son attended the 99th Street school. Since starting there, not only had he developed epilepsy but he had also required two surgeries for urethral strictures. Gibbs began talking to others on her street and found that they, too, had experienced an unusual number of serious "unexplained" illnesses in their families, besides sinking foundations, basement seepage, and burned-out gardens and yard vegetation. Then, after she and neighbor Debbie Cerrillo attended an August 1978 meeting at which the New York health commissioner declared an "emergency" in the area, they called residents to a gathering at the fire station. Hundreds of people showed up and they formed the Love Canal Homeowners Association (LCHA), electing Gibbs as president, Cerrillo as treasurer, and Karen Schroeder as secretary.[46]

In response to the activists' advocacy and protest, government officials eventually declared a federal health emergency, closed the 99th Street school, prepared a plan to purchase the inner ring of homes (later expanded to include the temporary relocation of seven hundred outer-ring families), and initiated a cleanup plan similar to the one recommended by the original consulting firm. By 1981, more than five hundred families had abandoned the area, and the Griffon Manor housing project on the neighborhood's western edge was half empty. Within a decade, however, the Love Canal Area Revitalization Agency declared parts of town "habitable" again. To help cover costs for the toxic waste removal and cleanup, Judge John Curtin ordered Hooker Chemical Company's successor, the Occidental Petroleum Corporation, to pay $98 million to New York State, and they settled with the federal government for $129 million as well, in addition to payouts from individual lawsuits filed by residents.[47]

The LCHA's success was due, of course, in no small part to the bold and persistent efforts of homemaker residents like Lois Gibbs, but the organization was also greatly aided by the support of (mostly male) local union members and their unions. The United Auto Workers represented employees at the General Motors plant in both Buffalo and Niagara Falls and already had a record of concern with environmental issues, including toxic chemicals in the workplace, and Love Canal resident and GM employee Edmund Pozniak had little trouble sparking interest among UAW rank-and-file and leadership. Similarly, the Oil, Chemical, and Atomic Workers (OCAW) union had long been committed to identifying the dangers of chemical compounds as well as demanding precautionary measures and negotiating higher pay to compensate for higher risks. In fact, Goodyear employee and OCAW member Harry Gibbs, married to Lois, was among those who helped bring their unions into the fight.[48]

During the winter of 1979, organized labor's concern about workplace chemical exposure led to the creation of the West New York Council on Occupational Safety and Health, which subsequently held a conference at the Buffalo Convention Center attended by over three hundred workers. In the months to follow, the UAW, OCAW, and the United Steelworkers donated members' time as well, union hall meeting space, and substantial funding to the LCHA, while profiling the residents' fight in their respective newsletters and journals. As frustrations with the state cleanup mounted, union men stoked the urge for militancy too, calling for direct action like picket lines and even violence, and in April 1979 Hooker Chemical Company employee Michael Bayliss leaked a damning internal corporate report to the press. The report revealed a history of chemical releases, the company's awareness of their potential effects, and its intention to hide information about the releases from employees and the public.[49]

Less integrally connected to the LCHA were residents at the federal housing project on the former canal's edge. They were predominantly black women, single heads of households, typically marginalized by race, class, and gender and by the fact of being renters, which excluded them from the homeowners' organization. Their situation was challenging because they needed government assistance to rent, yet other public housing in the area was filled nearly to capacity and few developments had large units to accommodate extended families. To help them organize and articulate their demands, the residents turned to the local branch of the National Association for the Advancement of Colored People (NAACP).[50]

William Abram, Sr., the Niagara Falls NAACP president, who had lived with his family at Griffon Manor during most of the 1960s and remembered constant odors as well as prevalent birth defects, eagerly stepped forward to get the chapter involved. Encouraged by that support, in late September 1978 the women formed their own group, the Concerned Love Canal Renters Association (CLCRA), initially led by Eelene Thorton and later Sarah Herbert. They pressed for financial aid to anyone who wanted to move, but Love Canal Task Force official Mike Cuddy rejected that demand, claiming there was "no medical justification" for it. When the state in turn announced a plan for purchasing homes of the neighborhood's remaining (white) residents, one that conspicuously omitted renters, CLCRA member Barbara Smith denounced it for being racist and discriminating against the poor. "The tenants are not excluded from the negative effects of chemical contamination," she argued, so the plan should be "for all residents."[51]

Blocked by state officials from protecting themselves and their families, as the 1970s came to a close Griffon Manor activists started working with the Ecumenical Task Force (ETF). This was a predominantly white, middle-class organization, including Catholics, Protestants, and Jews, formed in direct response to the Love Canal situation by Dr. Paul Moore, a Presbyterian minister from a nearby town. Moore believed that a Christian was obligated both to be a "responsible steward of this good earth" and to work for "a social order grounded in justice," part of an eternal covenant with God, but what the Hooker Chemical Company did in Niagara Falls had violated God's law, making an "ecological disaster" as well as a "human tragedy." This belief informed the group's five main goals: "providing direct aid to residents, assuming the advocate role in applying political pressure, gathering and interpreting appropriate data, seeking reconciliation through justice, [and] advocating the complete neutralization of toxic wastes." After hiring Sister Margeen Hoffmann to serve as executive director in the spring of 1979, the ETF began actively assisting the public housing residents to find other homes, initially placing some in local motels and arranging medical tests for them there. The activists were also particularly helpful with lobbying local politicians and exposing white city council members' racist reasons for opposing relocation, the chief one being that African Americans would be placed in neighborhoods that had historically been all white or nearly all white. As a result of ETF efforts, in 1981 Griffon Manor residents were finally included in the LCARA plan, and most of them moved away. Later, in 1986, as part of the area's final remediation, the building was razed and those who remained left as well.[52]

"NOT A RANDOM OCCURRENCE"

Just days after the first network news story about Love Canal, during the summer of 1978, farmers in the central part of rural North Carolina reported an oily odor on the shoulders of various state highways. Investigators quickly determined that the odor was coming from PCB-laden liquid waste, illegally dumped over a two-week period by Robert Burns and his two sons. Robert Ward, who owned the Ward Transformer Company in Raleigh, had hired Burns to do the dumping, to avoid following new regulatory requirements governing hazardous waste disposal under the Toxic Substances Control Act passed two years before. Eventually, Burns was sentenced to five months in jail, while the sentences for his two sons were suspended, and Ward was held liable for remediation costs. But as historian Eileen McGurty explains, this was not yet the end of the matter. Once the state had cleaned up the mess, officials devised a plan to construct a landfill to hold the contaminated soil, and they found a farmer facing bankruptcy near Afton, in Warren County, who agreed to sell his property for the site.[53]

Nearby residents worried about the threat the landfill would pose to groundwater as well as future economic development, organized opposition to the move, launching another decade-long battle that, together with the fight over toxic waste in New York, activists and others regard as the beginning of an "environmental justice" movement. On the one hand, Warren County was one of the poorest in the state, only third from the bottom (it slipped to the very bottom within a few years), and many locals believed they were selected for the landfill because of their assumed powerlessness. On the other hand, the majority of the county's population was African American, and black residents insisted that the siting constituted "environmental racism," a case of systematic disregard for their health and welfare because of race. Meanwhile, mainstream environmental organizations were conspicuous by an almost complete absence from the campaign, testament to their narrow definition of environmental problems as well as a clear preference for "beltway" pragmatism, and further demonstrating the need for a "grassroots" alternative.[54]

Initially, from 1979 to 1982, Warren County residents focused simply on stopping the landfill's construction, mustering every conceivable argument against the project in endless public hearings and separate meetings with state officials. Taking the lead in this were Ken and Deborah Ferruccio, who established a group called Concerned Citizens, most of whose members were white. When they failed, and the site was finished and ready to receive waste, activists shifted their attention to hindering its use and began working more closely with African American allies. Ken Ferruccio met with Reverend Luther Brown, the pastor at Coley Springs Baptist Church, located only a mile from the landfill, and Reverend Leon White, a United Church of Christ (UCC) minister and member of the UCC's Commission for Racial Justice, to discuss the need for direct action. Subsequently, on September 15, 1982, when the first trucks began hauling contaminated soil to the landfill, protesters marched from Reverend Brown's church to block the entrance, facing off against nearly one hundred state troopers, a National Guard battalion, and a helicopter. That day ended with sixty-seven arrests, and over the next two months, as more soil arrived and the protests continued, arrests mounted, numbering more than five hundred before the end. Once initial deliveries to the site were completed, it became clear that rainwater had saturated the soil, delaying the landfill's final capping. To protest the state's mishandling of the problem, Ken Ferruccio and several other activists blocked the access road and removed a pipe from the leachate collection system. They were arrested, but Ferruccio refused bail and began a nineteen-day hunger strike.[55]

One of the other participants in the landfill protests was Benjamin Chavis, born and raised in nearby Oxford, North Carolina. As a young man in the early 1970s he had been part of a civil rights campaign in Wilmington that led to a wrongful conviction for fire bombing a white-owned grocery store, followed by several years in jail. Fortunately, the governor shortened his sentence and a federal court reversed the conviction, allowing Chavis to leave prison in 1980, after which he became involved in the Warren County campaign and served as director of the UCC Commission for Racial Justice. Under his watch, the commission drafted a momentous report, *Toxic Wastes and Race in the United States*, published in 1987, linking social inequity to environmental risk.[56]

The authors of *Toxic Wastes and Race* had surveyed 415 hazardous waste sites in operation in 1986 as well as closed or abandoned sites identified by the Environmental Protection Agency, which they matched with demographic statistics. "The results of the study," they wrote, "suggest that the disproportionate numbers of racial and ethnic persons residing in communities with commercial hazardous waste facilities is not a random occurrence, but rather a consistent pattern." At the press conference where they released the report, Chavis used the term "environmental racism," and that became the cornerstone for building a national environmental justice movement. Later, the concept was more broadly defined to refer to the long-standing, systematic exclusion of people of color and their particular interests from mainstream environmental organizations as well, identifying the Sierra Club, Environmental Defense Fund, and others as obstacles to change. "Racism," activists declared in an open letter to the so-called Group of Ten, "is the root cause of your inaction around addressing environmental problems in our communities."[57]

Generally ignored by the traditional environmental movement, the new generation of activists had to depend on themselves to move a social environmental justice agenda forward. Key to this was the First National People of Color Environmental Leadership Summit, organized by the UCC in October 1991, which Chavis opened by highlighting the Warren County protests and which concluded with a formal declaration of environmental justice principles. The preamble for the declaration called on "all peoples of color to fight the destruction and taking of our lands and communities" and "to promote economic alternatives which would contribute to the development of environmentally safe livelihoods." The listed principles spoke to the particular concerns that led participants to the meeting, among them demands for an end to hazardous waste and radioactive materials as well as accountability for polluters and compensation for victims. Demonstrating a nuanced understanding of environmental contemporary problems, the declaration also affirmed "the right of all workers to a safe and healthy work environment without being forced to choose between an unsafe livelihood and unemployment." By each of these parts and as a whole, the declaration was a momentous document. Thirty years before, when she published *Silent Spring,* Rachel Carson had ignored both race and class as factors determining people's exposure to environmental hazards, or as variables to consider for protecting people's health, but the long history of environmentalism had finally cohered in a plainly articulated acknowledgment of that fact as well as a high-profile, nationally connected movement.[58]

Conclusion

"They Keep Threatening Us with the Loss of Our Jobs"

Although *Silent Spring* largely neglected to mention the important social dimensions underlying chemical pesticide application and exposure, notably avoiding any explicit discussion of race and class, the book occasionally called out the chemical industry for knowingly placing profits over environmental quality and human health. At different points in several chapters Carson deftly questioned the wisdom of poisoning the natural world in the name of so-called progress, and in a conclusion she painstakingly presented an overview of alternative biological controls. "Through all these new, imaginative, and creative approaches to the problem of sharing our earth with other creatures there runs a constant theme," she wrote, "the awareness that we are dealing with life—with living populations and all their pressures and counter-pressures, their surges and recessions." The old ways, "conceived in arrogance," were "as crude as the cave man's club," Carson insisted, while the alternatives began with humility and sought "to achieve a reasonable accommodation between the insect hordes and ourselves."[1] This final indictment put otherwise confident pesticide advocates on the defensive, and their response was swift, far-reaching, and often harsh. Over the next few months and years, the National Agricultural Chemicals Association (NACA), the Manufacturing Chemists' Association (MCA), the Nutrition Foundation, and other trade groups spent hundreds of thousands of dollars and produced a steady stream of brochures, bulletins, and "fact kits" to regain the public's trust and keep new federal and state oversight at bay, while scientists, doctors, and journalists published a slew of articles defending chemical controls. Yet as biographer Linda Lear points out, science and logic were not on the industry's side, and lacking that, critics were left to attack Carson herself rather than directly address the intricate details of her actual argument.[2]

With little variation, most of those who joined the campaign against the *Silent Spring* author tended to question the capacity of women to understand and write about science. This became clear even before the book appeared in print, after parts of it were serialized in the *New Yorker.* "Miss Rachel Carson's reference to the selfishness of insecticide manufacturers probably reflects her Communist sympathies," one reader complained to the magazine, and as for insects, "isn't it just like a woman to be scared to death of a few little bugs!"[3] Similarly, in a letter to President Eisenhower, former secretary of agriculture Ezra Taft Benson pointed out that Carson was "probably a Communist" and a "spinster with no children," neither of which qualified her well to speak about genetics. Continuing in this vein, the day after *Silent Spring* came out a *Time* magazine review cited the author's "literary skill" for misguidedly "arousing readers," raising the specter of women's assumed inclination for passion over reason. Some scientists sympathized with her "love of wildlife," the review acknowledged, but they feared "her emotional and inaccurate outburst" for the harm it might do "by alarming the non-technical public."[4]

One apparently frustrated scientist, William J. Darby, who was head of the Department of Biochemistry and director of the Division of Nutrition at Vanderbilt University School of Medicine, even wrote an article for *Chemical & Engineering News* titled "Silence! Miss Carson." Displaying the muddled thinking his frustration had induced, Darby quite inaccurately described *Silent Spring*'s sources as "organic gardeners, the antifluoride leaguers, the worshippers of 'natural foods' and those who cling to the vital principle, and other pseudo-scientists and faddists." Setting the author's supposedly questionable scientific qualifications against "those of our distinguished scientific leaders and statesmen," he advised, "this book should be ignored."[5] Harvard Medical School faculty and Nutrition Foundation member Frederick J. Stare also suggested that Carson had abandoned "scientific truth and proof for exaggeration," and he claimed there was nothing in her book that justified calling her a scientist. And following these public critiques, chemical companies hired a public relations firm to continue the attacks, led largely by American Cyanamid biochemist Robert White-Stevens, doing all that they could to brand their nemesis as "a fanatic leader of the cult of the balance of nature."[6]

In the face of this barrage Rachel Carson lobbied Houghton Mifflin to mount an advertising campaign of their own, but the publisher's budget was no match for the chemical industry's deeper pockets. Their first response, in the early part of 1963, was an advertisement quoting nine "unsolicited" and "un-paid" scientists who praised the book and warning readers that criticism "which makes light of the dangers of chemical poisons may emanate from sources dependent on the expanding use of chemicals." In addition, later that year Houghton Mifflin produced a pamphlet, "The Story of *Silent Spring*," setting true and false statements against one another and including a section titled "Is the Author Qualified?" After seeing the first draft, Carson rewrote that section and added to it, concluding with the observation that her book's main purpose, "to direct attention to a situation of which the general public was largely unaware, has been realized, perhaps because of, more than in spite of, the attacks."[7]

Carson also stepped up public speaking engagements, despite feeling weary from the cancer that was spreading through her body and suffering acute chest pain from radiation treatments, using every event to defend herself and her book. "As you listen to the present controversy about pesticides," she told one audience, "I recommend you ask yourself—Who speaks?—And Why?"[8] Then in late March she received a press release for the CBS program "The Silent Spring of Rachel Carson," set to air in April, and the list of those interviewed, including Robert Whites-Stevens, brought her back to despondency. "The show," she wrote to a friend, "is weighted against me." As it turned out, however, this was far from the case. When the program finally aired, the selected interviews presented Carson as calm, dignified, and reasonable, while casting her adversaries as wild-eyed, excitable, and evasive, a contrast apparent to most if not all of the 10 to 15 million viewers who tuned in. In fact, it was probably this show, even more than the *New Yorker* articles and book, that made *Silent Spring* a "household name" and a touchstone for the mid-twentieth-century environmental movement.[9]

Still, the chemical industry's personal attack on Carson was just the beginning of attempts by trade groups, business associations, and individual companies to deflect criticism from environmentalists with false premises, and in this way *Silent Spring* (or the reaction to it) does actually explain environmentalism. The industry's response to the book modeled the efforts other corporations and their allies later made to fracture and confuse the movement as a whole. They did this primarily by advancing the idea that Americans had to choose between "jobs" and "environment." Economic prosperity and environmental health were mutually exclusive, they insisted, and the costs of more carefully managing their use of resources, improving workplace safety, or regulating waste disposal, would force them to scale back production or shut down altogether.

Often enough the ruse worked, and for much of the twentieth century and into the next, corporations continued to maintain that they were too pressed by the stark reality of economic demands to take responsibility for the social and environmental costs their particular enterprise created. They also persistently promoted the idea that working people themselves were (or should be) too worried about losing their jobs to be environmental advocates. This was despite plenty of compelling evidence to the contrary, of course, including the various ways in which workers and unions associated with the industries most detrimental to the nation's air and water (auto, coal, chemicals, and the like) had contributed to the American environmental movement. It was believable enough, however, to sow distrust among activists and, just as importantly, to nudge labor and other social justice environmentalism out of common historical memory.

The main reason for the "jobs vs. environment" campaign's effectiveness was a new economic and political context. By the mid- to late 1970s, the American economy was plagued by "stagflation," an unusual combination of high unemployment and high inflation caused in part by a so-called energy crisis, a shortage of oil to meet rising demand that was exacerbated when the Organization of Arab Petroleum Exporting Countries imposed an embargo. All of this brought profound economic worries and woes to working people, making them (especially white men) vulnerable to a narrowing social and political perspective. Conservative political leaders who were part of a "New Right" used the moment to nurture a cultural backlash, stoking fears about racial equality and women's empowerment, and their efforts culminated with Ronald Reagan's election to the White House in 1980.

President Reagan not only held the line against a "rights revolution" but also oversaw deep cuts in federal spending (except in the military), tax relief for the rich, deregulation and lax regulatory enforcement, and a war on unions (starting with a mass firing of striking air traffic controllers). Employers took advantage of economic troubles as well as the political rightward swing by emphasizing the common interest workers supposedly had with them in fighting threats to their profit margins, including debilitating legislation to prevent air and water pollution. At the same time, mainstream environmental organizations like those grouped together as the "Group of Ten" continued to misunderstand and dismiss labor and community activists waging campaigns in which social, economic, and environmental concerns were inextricably linked. In some cases, they merely practiced benign neglect and in others they engaged in willful obstruction, neither of which aided a coherent and robust response to the New Right's class war, rhetorical or otherwise.

"WE LIVE WHERE THE COAL IS MINED"

One of the environmental campaigns where the "jobs vs. environment" pitch and the limitations of mainstream environmental organizations were on prominent display was the fight against surface coal mining in southern Appalachia. Although at the mid-twentieth century the United Mine Workers of America (UMW) was a corrupt and unresponsive organization, rank-and-file members of the union played a central role in that fight. During the 1960s, they joined their neighbors who were demanding state regulation and improved enforcement of control laws and then, when that proved to be futile, calling for outright abolition. This shift coincided with the rise of a dissident reform movement within the UMW, a bold attempt to challenge the sitting leadership, not coincidentally led by the very same members who were most outspoken about the problems with stripping. When the reform candidates finally swept the union's national elections in 1972, it seemed as if the United Mine Workers was on track to officially embrace labor environmentalism. Unfortunately, the country's declining economy, budding energy crisis, and unabated political shift to the right made it increasingly difficult for the new UMW leaders to stay the course. Besides that, mainstream environmental groups, namely the Sierra Club and the Environmental Policy Center, schemed to undermine the fight for abolition, opening the way for the coal industry to hijack federal regulatory hearings and dilute subsequent control legislation.

The immediate origin of the UMW dissident movement was a concerted effort by rank-and-file members to draw more attention to "black lung," a debilitating and often fatal disease that plagued many but was long ignored by coal companies, state and federal governments, and the union. Frustrated with the inaction, mineworkers in West Virginia established the Black Lung Association (BLA), and in February 1969 they called a statewide wildcat strike (one not officially sanctioned by the union). This forced the state legislature to pass a black lung bill, which became the model for the federal Coal Mine Health and Safety Act, and that in turn became the model for the Occupational Safety and Health Act (OSHA), passed in 1970, marking a great victory for the decades-old industrial hygiene movement.

As that was playing out, union activists began to organize a direct challenge to Tony Boyle, the UMW's corrupt president, backing Pennsylvania district leader Jock Yablonski for president in the 1969 elections. Although Boyle won the contest by a huge margin, the Department of Labor investigated and found widespread irregularities in the balloting and quickly ordered a new election. Before that could happen, however, union officials close to Boyle had Yablonski, his wife, and daughter murdered in their Washington, Pennsylvania, home. At the funeral, grieving supporters created Miners for Democracy (MFD), and at a meeting to write a platform as well as choose a slate of candidates for the next election, more than 450 delegates selected Boone County mineworker and BLA president Arnold Miller to lead the renewed struggle.

In addition to the critical part he played in the black lung campaign, Miller was known for rallying fellow dissidents to join West Virginia's growing campaign against strip mining, in counterpoint to United Mine Workers District 31 president L.J. Pnakovich and other union officials who ardently defended stripping. At an informational meeting sponsored by Citizens to Abolish Strip Mining in the early part of 1971, for example, Miller joined the panel discussion, flanked by Ivan White, another Boone County miner and black lung activist as well as a House of Delegates member, and many mineworkers eventually heeded their call to organize "massive demonstrations" and lobby for a ban. In February, dozens of deep miners visited the capitol building in

Charleston to talk to their representatives and advocate for an abolition law, declaring quite explicitly that the UMW leadership did not reflect their sentiments on the question and angrily confronting Pnakovich when they saw spotted him in the rotunda.[10] Two months later, in April, Miller, White, and retired coal miner Clarence Pauley traveled to Washington, D.C., to participate in a panel and hearings organized by West Virginia representative Ken Hechler, who had introduced the earlier health and safety legislation and was steadily gaining support for his bill to abolish surface coal mining. By May he had eighty-seven co-sponsors in the House, while Senators Gaylord Nelson and George McGovern had introduced an identical bill in the Senate.[11]

Observing the gathering momentum for the outlawing of stripmining, including the deepening and spreading support among miners, the coal industry responded strategically and modified its earlier position on regulation. Three years before, not only had the American Mining Congress (AMC) rejected all three proposed federal control bills, but Consolidation Coal vice president James Riley had railed against environmentalists at the trade group's annual convention, calling them "stupid idiots, socialists and commies who don't know what they are talking about."[12] In September 1971, however, fearing that unwavering resistance to any oversight would make abolition even more likely, the AMC board of directors adopted a statement favoring "realistic surface mining regulation at the state level" as well as "federal surface mining legislation which is realistically designed to assist the states and the surface mining industry ... so as to have to the least practicable adverse effect on other resource values."[13] The United Mine Workers also officially retreated from wholesale rejection of control laws to support minimal federal legislation. "State regulations have failed," UMW president Tony Boyle announced—contradicting much of what he had said just two years before—"and there has been lack of adequate standards and enforcement by the states."[14] Yet overall, union leaders remained adamantly opposed to the abolition of coal surface mining, which they described as "sheer nonsense," "so much political grandstanding," a "preservationist pipe-dream," and a threat to "badly needed jobs and essential electric power."[15]

Ironically, back in the coalfields Miners for Democracy organizers began to hedge on a ban too, hoping to get the increasing number of surface mine members to support their insurgency. On the eve of the election, the organization drafted a platform with a plank that was largely the creation of Bill Kelley, president of Local Union 7690, a strip mine local in eastern Ohio. The plank stressed "BOTH jobs and land," insisting that nonunion surface mineworkers would be unionized and reclamation laws enforced. "We live where the coal is mined," Kelley declared, "and we're the ones with the most at stake if we don't have good laws and a strong union to see that they get enforced."[16]

Ultimately, this and other campaign outreach efforts were effective enough that Miller, along with the MFD candidates for vice president and secretary-treasurer, won the election in December, though narrowly.[17] The next year, when Congress held more hearings, the newly installed president forwarded a statement in support of both strong federal regulation and selective abolition, reflecting conflicting and evolving views within the UMW. But he respectfully declined to endorse any of the pending bills, since the union had not been able to agree on any one in particular.[18] In fact, as surface miners assumed ever more influence in the union, the debate shifted away from the question of a ban and back to the question of whether there should be any federal oversight at all. The UMW finally endorsed a specific bill in 1974, yet only after a heated special session of the executive board in which Miller cast a tie-breaking vote. "Everyone accepted the need to protect the jobs of our members," he delicately explained, "while protecting areas where our members and families live."[19]

Simultaneous with the emergence of ominous division in the United Mine Workers, serious fractures developed among strip mining activists more generally. Soon after groups from the mountain region established the Appalachian Coalition to advocate nationally for a ban, representatives from several national environmental groups met in the Washington, D.C., office of Friends of the Earth and formed the National Coalition against Strip Mining (NACSM), which did not officially favor abolition. Louise Dunlap, who went to work for the newly established Environmental Policy Center, chaired NACSM, and she and Peter Borelli, the eastern representative for the Sierra Club, began colluding behind the scenes, strategizing in private correspondence and conversations to emphasize the problems with outlawing strip mining and promote regulatory standards instead. Testifying before a congressional committee in 1973, Borelli explained that the positions of his organization and the coal industry were not really that far apart. "We wholeheartedly agree that a balance, of course, is necessary if our economy and environment is to coexist," he said, "and I know of no other social arrangement that has worked in this country."[20] Consequently, support for the House and Senate abolition bills began to wither away. When Representative Hechler's assistant called Senator Ted Kennedy's office to discuss co-sponsoring, a legislative aide told him "they were backing off because [Senator]

Nelson's office had told them Nelson was backing off." The reason for this turnabout, he elaborated, was that "they felt the environmentalists weren't seriously pushing the abolition bill anymore."[21]

Seeing the threat of abolition dissipate, in 1975 the coal industry went back to advocating only the most minimal regulatory controls, pressing the concern for jobs as their primary rationale. When House and Senate committees reported out more regulatory bills for floor debate, surface mine operators helped send a huge caravan of coal haulers to D.C. to lobby members of Congress as well as President Ford. Drivers adorned their trucks with painted slogans and banners denouncing the bills, such as "H.R. 25—We Don't Need Another 25,000 Unemployed" and "Mr. President Save Our Jobs—Veto Bill 25 & Bill 7." As they idled near the White House, industry representatives met with federal energy administrator Frank Zarb, who told them that both he and Ford were sympathetic to their concerns.[22]

Later, when the House and Senate passed the bills and they were reconciled, the President promptly vetoed the legislation. In his veto message, he highlighted the concern that the regulatory act would put up to 36,000 Americans out of work, raise utility bills, make the nation more dependent on foreign oil, and reduce coal production in the midst of an energy crisis. Frank Zarb said much the same, including claims that whole counties in Appalachia would see their local economies destroyed and tens of millions of tons of coal reserves would be closed to extraction by various protective restrictions. Meanwhile, the American Mining Congress and other trade groups went on the offensive, declaring that the vetoed bills were littered with "unrealistic and unworkable provisions" and insisting that properly enforced state laws were sufficient. The United Mine

Workers came back into line as well, officially retreating from a push for federal legislation and going on record in support of reclamation laws being enacted on a state-by-state basis, a position the recommendation committee insisted was needed "so that we will not put anyone out of work."[23]

The end result of all the compromising was the Surface Mining Control and Reclamation Act (SMCRA), signed into law in 1977 despite pleas from Appalachian activists to President Carter to veto the bill. Similar to earlier proposals made by the coal industry, SMCRA essentially legalized the destruction caused by strip mining. It was lacking in many ways, including no steep slope limitations and no requirement for surface owner consent or compensation, and it did little to ensure that enforcement would be any better than the inadequate efforts at the state level in preceding years. The law also opened the way to a new form of surface extraction called "mountaintop removal," in which operators leveled whole mountains to get at coal seams below, filling nearby valleys with the "overburden" and constructing huge impoundments to contain toxic slurry waste. This type of mining was devastating to the landscape, and while it enabled record-high levels of production, it caused record-low levels of employment, further decimating the United Mine Workers member ranks.

Oddly, though, the union leadership blamed "environmentalists," blithely ignoring the far more important role that multinational energy conglomerates now played in bringing them down. Demonstrating a profound historical amnesia and registering just how strongly their vision had been influenced by divisive corporate rhetoric, at a 1999 rally to protest a judge's recent decision against a coal company for violating the Clean Water Act, which prompted the company to unnecessarily lay off thirty employees, UMW president Cecil Roberts declared that mine workers had been "kicked in the teeth again by the environmental community."[24] More than a decade later, Roberts was still at the helm, holding the union steadfast against the Environmental Protection Agency's announced plan to reduce greenhouse gas emissions, parroting the same small-minded sentiment as coal industry trade groups: "This is simply a recipe for disaster in America's coalfields," he declared, "especially in the eastern coalfields."[25]

"THE EYES AND EARS OF THE COMMUNITY"

Although the campaign against surface coal mining painfully showed how social justice–minded labor environmentalism could falter, there were other cases in the 1970s and 1980s that demonstrated its persistent promise. One of these involved the Oil, Chemical, and Atomic Workers (OCAW) union, which, along with the United Farm Workers, represented many of the men and women most directly affected by the toxic and radioactive hazards singled out by Rachel Carson for the apocalyptic threat they posed to the modern age. As with the UFW and the United Auto Workers, the OCAW's environmental engagement was due in part to a forward-thinking leader, Tony Mazzochi, who had been weaned on radical politics while growing up in Brooklyn. During the 1950s, when he was serving on the union's executive board, he befriended Barry Commoner, a fellow Brooklyn native and radical who used his faculty position at Washington University in St. Louis to establish and coordinate the Committee for Nuclear Information (and who later went on to aid local lead activists). Commoner helped enlarge Mazzochi's social and environmental awareness, and by the time he was the OCAW legislative director in the 1960s he was fully committed to transforming the union into a formidable environmental organization in its own right. His strategy, as biographer Les Leopold explains, was to leverage demands for a federal occupational health and safety law to raise rank-and-file consciousness and build bridges with other environmental activists.[26]

Mazzochi launched his effort by pushing a resolution at the OCAW national convention in 1967, inviting consumer advocate Ralph Nader to speak about why protective legislation was more important than ever before. Occupational dangers had changed, he told delegates, from simple injuries with immediate consequences to toxic exposures that often had only latent consequences. Mazzochi said much the same in smaller meetings at union locals, often accompanied by medical doctors and scientists, and he made the point central to his road show, "Hazards in the Industrial Environment," which debuted in the spring of 1969 at a Holiday Inn in Kenilworth, New Jersey. "Though we've talked about health and safety for a long time," he told the more than two hundred OCAW district leaders and chemical workers present, "the emphasis had been on the safety of it." Their industry harbored a more "insidious" danger, however, "the danger of the contaminated environment ... something we don't feel, see or smell, and of which most of us become contemptuous, simply because it does not affect us immediately."[27]

In meeting after meeting, as workers testified to their own local struggles with uncooperative company officials, Mazzochi also insisted that exposing dangers in the workplace was a critical step toward recognizing environmental problems beyond factory and refinery gates, since those problems typically began in the workplace and spread outward. In much the same way that UAW members were concerned about air and water pollution around their plants and dissident mine workers worried about the environmental effects of surface mining in surrounding hills and hollows, the OCAW rank-and-file audience grasped the connections between the environmental dangers they faced at work and the environmental hazards people faced beyond. "Not only do we suffer from these fumes in the plant," Woodbridge Chemical employee Harold Smith acknowledged, "but the people in the community around our plant suffer. That means that somebody else's kid is inhaling these fumes when he wakes up in the morning."[28]

What little protection OCAW rank-and-file had at work was limited to the Walsh-Healy Act, a law that established workplace exposure standards according to *The Documentation of Threshold Values*, published by the American Conference of Governmental Industrial Hygienists (ACGIH). Despite its name, the ACGIH was in fact sponsored by private industry, and the committees that set exposure limits, which included management representatives but no one from labor, did so with no outside review or opportunity for appeal. Not surprisingly, the standards were weak, and they covered only five hundred chemicals, leaving twenty thousand others with no guidelines. Additionally, Walsh-Healy Act coverage was limited to companies with large government contracts, and provisions for inspections allowed advance notice and denied union officials the right to know the results. "In short," Les Leopold argues, "chemical companies ruled as absolute monarchs over chemical production, exposure, and regulation."[29]

Buoyed by coal miners' success in passing the Coal Mine Safety and Health Act, however, OCAW and other unions pressed harder for more comprehensive legislation, which they accomplished in 1970 with enactment of the Occupational Safety and Health Act. The new law required all employers,

irrespective of industry, to provide a workplace "free from recognized hazards that are causing or likely to cause death or serious physical harm," gave organized labor the right to petition
the secretary of labor for new or improved standards, and set up
a protocol for record keeping, unannounced inspections, and
federal enforcement. OSHA also created the National Institute
of Occupational Safety and Health to conduct research and
education, building on a whole century's worth of industrial
hygiene studies, recommendations, and interventions, many of
which proved to be pioneering investigations of substances and
emissions that caused widespread harm.[30]

Following the legislative victory, Mazzochi turned more of
his attention to the oil industry, which, like the chemical industry, had a dismal health and safety record. This was something
he wanted the OCAW to address during negotiations for a
national refinery contract, and he presented a case for going
beyond OSHA requirements. Once union officials sat down at
the bargaining table, they decided to ask for a joint Labor-Man-
agement Health and Safety Committee with the power to make
binding recommendations, periodic company-paid plant inspections by independent and mutually agreed upon health experts,
company-paid medical examinations for all employees by
OCAW-approved doctors, and full disclosure of morbidity and
mortality data. All of the largest oil producers eventually
accepted the terms by the end of 1972, with the exception of Shell
Oil, whose intransigence triggered a walkout by five thousand
workers. Drawing on the outreach work Mazzochi had been
doing for the past few years, the union received support from
eleven major environmental organizations as well, including
members' participation on picket lines and a coordinated Shell
boycott. "If toxic substances are present in oil refineries," the

newly formed environmental alliance announced, "they most assuredly are spreading outside the plant walls to neighboring communities." The struggle illustrated the "shared concerns of workers and environmentalists," they continued, and "we support the efforts of the OCAW in demanding a better environment, not just for its own workers, but for all Americans."[31]

In the end, the Shell Oil strike and boycott were not entirely successful, with the company hedging on certain aspects of the original demands, but compromising did not undermine industry-wide pattern bargaining as union leaders had feared. Additionally, the walkout motivated the OCAW to pressure OSHA for stricter standards on exposure to asbestos, radiation, mercury, benzene, and chemical pesticides, and it created the basis for at least some continued cooperation with environmental organizations, including the Sierra Club. "We have more in common than divides us," club president Mike McCloskey declared at the union's 1973 biennial convention. "We know that what is good for General Motors or Dow Chemical is not necessarily good for us all."[32]

Later, not too long after Tony Mazzochi was elected vice president and put in charge of health and safety as well as organizing, the OCAW flexed its labor environmental muscle again during a corporate campaign against MAPCO, which had purchased a Memphis refinery and immediately demanded major concessions from the workers. Rather than strike, the employees reached out to local residents as well as national environmental groups, emphasizing common concerns about air quality, illegal sludge burial, and groundwater contamination. They were, effectively, presenting themselves as the front line in uncovering environmental problems, not unlike what workers had been doing for the past century. "If there's a fight over jobs and the environment," campaign coordinator Richard Leonard explained, "you want the community to see the workers as important. You want the community to visualize the union as a necessity to allow workers to be able to speak up concerning these environmental or health and safety questions and to be the eyes and ears of the community, ideally."[33]

The ongoing labor community alliance was on most dramatic display, however, during its fight with German chemical giant BASF, at one of the company's plants in Louisiana's "Cancer Alley." After workers there refused major contract concessions in the summer of 1984, the company locked them out. OCAW sent Richard Miller, Mazzochi's assistant, to help fight back. He began by building a coalition of local civic and community groups, national environmental organizations, and the German Green Party. Together, they painted the company as an environmental outlaw, drawing on the personal knowledge and revelations of production and maintenance employees. Although it took a long time, nearly six years, this strategy was finally successful, winning an agreement that allowed all employees to return to the plant, established terms for improving working conditions, and spelled out plans for reducing BASF's environmental violations.[34] In the process, as happened during the Shell Oil strike and boycott, OCAW Local 4–620 members were transformed. "Five years ago," worker Bobby Schneider explained, "I felt if you wanted your job and you wanted to live in this state, you were just going to have to put up with it. I certainly don't feel that way today. There are ways to make these plants safe—to cut down on wastes, to recycle wastes, and to find proper ways to get rid of the waste that's left." Many if not all of them saw through corporate "jobs versus environment" rhetoric. "They keep threatening us with the loss of our jobs," worker John Diagle observed, "but we don't want those kinds of jobs anymore. We want clean jobs." Building on this raised consciousness, Local 4–620 launched Louisiana Workers against Toxic Health Hazards (LA WATCH), supported by a coalition of other unions and environmental groups and meant to assist workers concerned about environmental malpractice in the workplace.[35]

Still, even the OCAW could not completely avoid the prevailing economic and political forces at the century's end. Automation at refineries and elsewhere wiped out thousands of jobs, while the war against organized labor institutionalized by Ronald Reagan's ascendance to the White House in 1980 also had dramatic effects. Over the fifteen years from 1979 to 1994 the union's ranks shrank from 180,000 to 90,000, mirroring a larger national decline in union density (the proportion of the labor force belonging to unions), from a high of 35 percent in the mid-1950s to 12.5 percent by the 1990s. For the OCAW, this meant a steep drop in dues even as administrative costs went up. Like other unions, they dealt with the decline by merging with another union, the United Rubber Workers, which had also seen a drop in membership, from 190,000 in 1974 to 100,000 by 1993.

Meanwhile, not so paradoxically, the majority of environmental organizations grew in number, members, and total revenue. They saw steady but small membership growth from the end of World War II to 1970, when the total number reached 1 million. By the time the "New Right" revolution was in full swing in the early 1980s, that number had increased to 5.1 million, then to 8.3 million in 1990 and 15.9 million in 1999. A few select groups also saw an astounding increase in their budgets. In 1965, according to Mark Dowie, the ten largest environmental organizations operated on less than $10 million, but thirty years later the "Washington-based mainstream sector of the movement," about twenty-four different organizations, had a total budget of more than $500 million. Certainly, by these and other measures, at the start of the twenty-first century the fate of organized labor and the fortunes of environmental groups were no longer linked, and mainstream environmentalists were the clear beneficiaries of the varied destinies.[36]

While the spread of environmental consciousness and activism seems to be exhibiting no signs of abating in the near term, much of what we call the "environmental movement" in America is hobbled by the story we tell about its origins. With all due respect to Rachel Carson and the lifelong effort she made to raise people's awareness about imminent threats to the natural world, the widely held and often-repeated notion that the movement started with the publication of *Silent Spring* in 1962 is profoundly inadequate. Most importantly, it limits what we consider to be "environmentalism" and confuses who counts as an "environmentalist." Failing to acknowledge the movement's deeper roots and push our historical perspective back to the start of industrial capitalism in the early nineteenth century, and then to bring that perspective forward into the twentieth century, we cannot see how labor exploitation and environmental degradation were two aspects of the same dramatic transformation. We also miss the pioneering role that organized labor, dissident union members, and unaffiliated workers played in calling attention to both at the same time. Likewise, by ignoring the many moments before the mid-twentieth century when African Americans and immigrants linked racial inequality and ethnic prejudice to pollution exposure and disparate public health impacts, we mistake "environmental justice" for a relatively new phenomenon. In turn, we give mainstream environmental groups an underserved pass for being so late to recognize the broader dimensions of environmental problems. Only when we fully reckon with all of these aspects and dimensions of American environmentalism's history— recovering them in pieces from the archives and assembling them together into a new narrative—can we build a movement with a true capacity to address the challenges we face in the present and future.

NOTES

INTRODUCTION

1. Linda Lear, *Rachel Carson: Witness for Nature* (New York: Henry Holt, 1997), 3, 419–21, 450–54.

2. March 1, 1963, *Detroit News,* Box 552, Folder 4, "Speeches, Mar. 1963," President's Office, Walter P. Reuther Collection, United Auto Workers, Archives of Labor and Urban Affairs, Wayne State University, Detroit, Michigan [hereafter cited as UAW President's Office Collection].

3. Transcript, Folder 3, "Speeches; Clear Water Conference, 6 Nov 1965," Box 555, UAW President's Office Collection.

4. Transript, Folder 6, "Speeches; Water Pollution Control Federation, 25 Sept 1968," Box 559, UAW President's Office Collection; Brief History of UAW Environmental Leadership—1948, Folder "Conservation & Recreation Depts. History, policies & operations, 1930s–1970s," Box 11, Conservation and Recreation Departments Collection, United Auto Workers, Archives of Labor and Urban Affairs, Wayne State University, Detroit, Michigan [hereafter cited as UAW Conservation and Recreation Departments Collection].

5. Nelson Lichtenstein, *Walter Reuther: The Most Dangerous Man in Detroit* (Urbana: University of Illinois Press, 1995), 436–37; John Kifner,

"Earth Day Group Zeros in on Autos: Students and Union Leaders See Air Pollution Peril," *New York Times,* July 20, 1970, 52.

6. Robert Gordon, "Environmental Blues: Working-Class Environmentalism and the Labor-Environment Alliance" (PhD diss., Wayne State University, 2004), 214–17; Chad Montrie, *A People's History of Environmentalism in the United States* (New York: Continuum, 2011), 107–8.

7. Lear, *Rachel Carson,* 4.

8. Thomas Dunlap, ed., *DDT, "Silent Spring," and the Rise of Environmentalism* (Seattle: University of Washington Press, 2008), jacket description.

9. Michelle Mart, "Rhetoric and Response: The Cultural Impact of Rachel Carson's *Silent Spring,*" *Left History* 14, no. 2 (2009): 31.

10. Gary Kroll, "The 'Silent Springs' of Rachel Carson: Mass Media and the Origins of Modern Environmentalism," *Public Understanding of Science* 10, no. 4 (2001): 416–17.

11. Mark Stoll, www.environmentandsociety.org/exhibitions/silent-spring/legacy-rachel-carsons-silent-spring, accessed November 7, 2015.

12. Eliza Griswold, "How 'Silent Spring' Ignited the Environmental Movement," *New York Times Magazine,* September 21, 2012.

13. Robin McKie, "Rachel Carson and the Legacy of *Silent Spring,*" *Guardian,* May 26, 2012.

14. Laurie Lawlor, illustrated by Laura Beingessner, *Rachel Carson and Her Book That Changed the World* (New York: Holiday House, 2012), 31.

15. Amy Ehrlich, illustrated by Wendell Minor, *Rachel: The Story of Rachel Carson* (New York: Silver Whistle, 2003), n.p.

16. Julia B. Corbett, "Women, Scientists, Agitators: Magazine Portrayal of Rachel Carson and Theo Colburn," *Journal of Communication* 51, no. 4 (2001): 724; Maril Hazlett, "'Woman vs. Man vs. Bugs': Gender and Popular Ecology in Early Reactions to Silent Spring," *Environmental History* 9, no. 4 (2004): 715; Lear, *Rachel Carson,* 4–5; Michael B. Smith, "'Silence, Miss Carson!' Science, Gender, and the Reception of *Silent Spring,*" *Feminist Studies* 27, no. 3 (2001): 733

17. Adam Rome, *The Genius of Earth Day: How a 1970 Teach-In Unexpectedly Made the First Green Generation* (New York: Hill and Wang, 2014), 9–10.

18. Kroll, "The 'Silent Springs' of Rachel Carson," 416; Mart, "Rhetoric and Response," 46, 48–49.

19. See particularly Samuel Hays, *Beauty, Health, and Permanence: Environmental Politics in the United States, 1955–1985* (New York: Cambridge University Press, 1987); Adam Rome, *The Bulldozer in the Countryside: Suburban Sprawl and the Rise of American Environmentalism* (New York: Cambridge University Press, [1994] 2001); and Christopher Sellers, *Crabgrass Crucible: Suburban Nature and the Rise of Environmentalism in Twentieth-Century America* (Chapel Hill: University of North Carolina Press, 2012).

20. John Cumbler, *Reasonable Use: The People, the Environment, and the State, New England 1790–1930* (New York: Oxford University Press, 2001), 114–18, 124–32; Bowditch quote, 115.

21. Lear, *Rachel Carson*, 423, 306; Rachel Carson, *Silent Spring* (Boston: Houghton Mifflin, [1962] 1987), 158–59.

22. Quotes are from Chad Montrie, *To Save the Land and People: A History of Opposition to Surface Coal Mining in Appalachia* (Chapel Hill: University of North Carolina Press, 2003), 33.

23. Montrie, *A People's History of Environmentalism*, 130–32.

24. Linda Nash, "The Fruits of Ill-Health: Pesticides and Workers' Bodies in Post–World War II California," *Osiris* 19 (2004): 205, 207; Laura Pulido, *Environmentalism and Economic Justice* (Tucson: University of Arizona Press, 1996), 77, 81; "Domestic Agricultural Migrants in the United States (1965)," Public Health Service Publication No. 540, Folder 1, "Farm Labor Migration Patterns, 1965–69," Box 13, United Farm Workers Information and Research Department Collection, United Farm Workers, Archives of Labor and Urban Affairs, Wayne State University, Detroit, Michigan [hereafter cited as UFW Information and Research Collection].

25. Montrie, *A People's History of Environmentalism*, 125; "Join the Non-Violent Strike for Justice" and "Pesticides: The Poisons We Eat," Folder 20, "Pesticides, Leaflets, n.d.," Box 21, United Farm Workers Administration Files Collection, Archives of Labor and Urban Affairs, Wayne State University, Detroit, Michigan [hereafter cited as UFW Administration Files Collection].

26. "Nora" to "Cesar," April 16, 1970, Folder 15, "Ecology Walk, 1969–1970," Box 6, United Farm Workers: Administration Files Collection,

Archives of Labor and Urban Affairs, Wayne State University, Detroit, Michigan.

27. Chris Meyer to Victoria A. Hays, August 24, 1973, Folder 21, "Environmental Action," Box 3, Work Department Collection, United Farm Workers, Archives of Labor and Urban Affairs, Wayne State University, Detroit, Michigan [hereafter cited as UFW Work Department Collection].

28. César Chávez to Brock Evans, May 9, 1973, ibid.

29. Charles Askins, "The South's Problem in Game Protection," *Recreation Magazine*, May 1909, quoted in William T. Hornaday, *Our Vanishing Wild Life: Its Extermination and Preservation* (New York: Charles Scribner's Sons, 1913), 110.

30. Colin Fisher, *Urban Green: Nature, Recreation, and the Working Class in Industrial Chicago* (Chapel Hill: University of North Carolina Press, 2015), 97.

31. *The Northwestern Bulletin* (Minneapolis), September 22, 1923, 1.

32. Robert Gioielli, *Environmental Activism and the Urban Crisis: Baltimore, St. Louis, Chicago* (Philadelphia: Temple University Press, 2014), 38–39, 54–55.

33. See Jacquelyn Dowd Hall, "The Long Civil Rights Movement and the Uses of the Past," *Journal of American History* 91, no. 4 (2005): 1233–63.

CHAPTER ONE. "I THINK LESS OF THE FACTORY
THAN OF MY NATIVE DELL"

1. Rachel Carson, *Silent Spring* (Boston: Houghton Mifflin, [1962] 1987), 3–4.

2. Ibid., 5–7, 16.

3. Brian Donohue, *The Great Meadow: Farmers and the Land in Colonial Concord* (New Haven: Yale University Press, 2004), 187–88 (quote, 187); Theodore Steinberg, *Nature Incorporated: Industrialization and the Waters of New England* (Amherst: University of Massachusetts Press, 1991), 141.

4. Donohue, *The Great Meadow*, 210.

5. John Cumbler, *Reasonable Use: The People, the Environment, and the State, New England 1790–1930* (New York: Oxford University Press, 2001), 63–64.

6. Steinberg, *Nature Incorporated,* 99–101.

7. Ibid., 31–32; Cumbler, *Reasonable Use,* 67.

8. Steinberg, *Nature Incorporated,* 161–62, 176.

9. Henry David Thoreau, *A Week on the Concord and Merrimack Rivers* (New York: Library of America, 1985), 28–29, 31; Donohue, *The Great Meadow,* 187.

10. "Everes," "American Forest Scenery," *Operatives' Magazine* 1 (April 1841): 1.

11. V.C.N., "A Morning Walk," *Operatives' Magazine* 3 (June 1841): 47.

12. Mary H. Blewett, ed., *Caught between Two Worlds: The Diary of a Lowell Mill Girl, Susan Brown, of Epsom, New Hampshire* (Lowell, Mass.: Lowell Museum, 1984), 14.

13. "Ella" [Harriet Farley], "A Weaver's Reverie," *Lowell Offering* 1 (1841): 188–89.

14. E.C.T., "Journey to Lebanon Springs," *Lowell Offering* 2 (1842): 191.

15. J.R., untitled letter, *Voice of Industry,* October 23, 1846, 4.

16. Betsy Chamberlain, "Recollections of My Childhood," *Lowell Offering* 1 (1841): 78–79.

17. "The Lowell Factory Girl" in *Factory Girls: A Collection of Writings on Life and Struggles in the New England Factories of the 1840s,* ed. Philip S. Foner (Urbana: University of Illinois Press, 1977), 6–9.

18. Lucy Larcom, *A New England Girlhood: Outline from Memory* (Boston: Northeastern University Press, [1889] 1986), 120–21, 182.

19. Cumbler, *Reasonable Use,* 54, 57–58; Lucius Ellsworth, *The American Leather Industry* (Chicago: Rand McNally, 1969), 5–8.

20. Cumbler, *Reasonable Use,* 52.

21. Chad Montrie, *A People's History of Environmentalism in the United States* (New York: Continuum, 2011), 30.

22. Josiah Curtis, *Brief Remarks on the Hygiene of Massachusetts, but More Particularly on the Cities of Boston and Lowell* (Philadelphia: T.K. and P.G. Collins, 1849), 35, 37.

23. David Daggett, "A Brief Account of a Trial at Law, in Which the Influence of Water Raised by a Mill-dam, on the Health of the Inhabitants in the Neighborhood Was Considered," *Memoirs of the Connecticut Academy of Arts and Sciences* (New Haven, 1813), vol. 1, pt. 1, no. 12, 131–34.

24. Cumbler, *Reasonable Use,* 109–10, 53, 62, 49.

25. Ibid., 112, 114.

26. Ibid., 111, 114–15.

27. Ibid., 117–18.

28. Ibid., 116–25; Steinberg, *Nature Incorporated,* 227–28, 235.

29. Robert Clarke, *Ellen Swallow Richards: The Woman Who Founded Ecology* (Chicago: Follett, 1973), 116, 145–48.

30. Ibid., 148. In an official history, published by the experiment station staff in 1953, Richards was absurdly listed as an "assistant" to Jordan. Raymond S. Patterson, *Proud Heritage: A Review of the Lawrence Experiment Station, Past, Present, and Future* (Boston: Massachusetts Department of Public Health, 1953), 12–16.

31. *The Report of the Lawrence White Fund: Studies in Relation to Lawrence Massachusetts, Made in 1911, under the Advice of Frances H. McLean by Robert E. Todd and Frank B. Sanborn at the Procurement of the Trustees of the White Fund* (Andover, Mass.: Andover Press, 1912), 217–20.

32. Steinberg, *Nature Incorporated,* 191.

33. Cumbler, *Reasonable Use,* 93.

34. Ibid., 95, 97.

35. Ibid., 170.

36. Karl Jacoby, *Crimes against Nature: Squatters, Poachers, Thieves, and the Hidden History of American Conservation* (Berkeley: University of California Press, 2001), 2–3. See also "Foreword" by Henry Fairfield Osborn in William T. Hornaday, *Our Vanishing Wild Life: Its Extermination and Preservation* (New York: Scribner, 1913), vii.

37. Jacoby, *Crimes against Nature,* 5–6; Richard Judd, *Common Lands, Common People: The Origins of Conservation in Northern New England* (Cambridge, Mass.: Harvard University Press, 1997), 123–24.

38. Jacoby, *Crimes against Nature,* 15–18.

39. Ibid., 23–26, 34–36.

40. Ibid., 39–44, 62.

41. Benjamin Heber Johnson, "Conservation, Subsistence, and Class at the Birth of Superior National Forest," *Environmental History* 4 (January 1999): 90.

42. Ibid., 89–90, 93.

43. Ibid., 94.

44. William Cronon, "The Trouble with Wilderness; or, Getting Back to the Wrong Nature," in *Uncommon Ground: Rethinking the Human Place in Nature*, ed. William Cronon (New York: W. W. Norton, 1996), 69–90.

45. H. Duane Hampton, *How the U.S. Cavalry Saved Our National Parks* (Bloomington: Indiana University Press, 1971), 137–38, 146, 148–49; Montrie, *A People's History of Environmentalism*, 36.

46. Mark David Spence, *Dispossessing the Wilderness: Indian Removal and the Making of the National Parks* (New York: Oxford University Press, 1999), 117, 124, 128.

47. Jacoby, *Crimes against Nature*, 90–91.

48. Ibid., 97–98 (Warren quote, 98), 99, 119; Richard A. Bartlett, *Yellowstone: A Wilderness Besieged* (Tucson: University of Arizona Press, 1985), 264; Montrie, *A People's History of Environmentalism*, 50–51.

CHAPTER TWO. "WHY DON'T THEY DUMP
THE GARBAGE ON THE BULLY-VARDS?"

1. Rachel Carson, *Silent Spring* (Boston: Houghton Mifflin, [1962] 1987), 85, 87, 90–91.

2. Ibid., 158–61.

3. Samuel Hays, *Beauty, Health, and Permanence: Environmental Politics in the United States, 1955–1985* (Cambridge: Cambridge University Press, 1987), 34.

4. Christopher C. Sellers, *Crabgrass Crucible: Suburban Nature and the Rise of American Environmentalism in the Twentieth Century* (Chapel Hill: University of North Carolina Press, 2012), 3, 256, 264. See also Adam Rome, *The Bulldozer in the Countryside: Suburban Sprawl and the Rise of American Environmentalism* (New York: Cambridge University Press, 2001).

5. Ten years after the first Long Island action against DDT, for example, with the resumption of spraying to control mosquitoes, attorney Victor Yannacone, Jr., teamed up with State University of New York biologist Charles F. Wurster, Jr., to lead a lawsuit that centered on the decline of the osprey population, and after forming the Environmental Defense Fund they achieved a statewide ban against the pesticide. During a 1971 House Committee on Agriculture

hearing to consider a federal ban, which might mean switching from chlorinated hydrocarbon to organophosphate pesticides (with unknown consequences), Representative John Rarick quoted Wurster: "It really doesn't make a lot of difference," he reportedly said, "because the organophosphate [pesticide] acts locally and only kills farm workers, and most of them are Mexicans and Negroes." See David Kinkela, *DDT and the American Century: Global Health, Environmental Politics, and the Pesticide That Changed the World* (Chapel Hill: University of North Carolina Press, 2011), 149–50.

6. Samuel Milton Jones, "Letter to Eugene V. Debs, September 25, 1900," in *Letters of Love and Labor* (Toledo, Ohio: Franklin Printing and Engraving Co., 1900), 90.

7. Samuel Milton Jones, *The New Right* (New York: N.O. Nelson, 1899), 139.

8. "Annual Report of the Board of Health, 1886," in *Annual Statement of the Finances of Toledo, the Mayor's Message, and Reports of the Various Municipal Departments* (Toledo, Ohio, 1886).

9. C.L. Van Pelt, "Municipal Sanitation," *The Sanitarian*, no. 199 (June 1886): 485–86.

10. "Mayor's Message, 1901," in *Annual Statement of the Finances of Toledo, the Mayor's Message, and Reports of the Various Municipal Departments* (Toledo, Ohio, 1901).

11. *Ordinance No. 498*, 1907, Chapter XI of Toledo Code; "Annual Report of the Board of Health, Year 1911," in *Annual Statement of the Finances of Toledo* (1911).

12. Judith Walzer Leavitt, *The Healthiest City: Milwaukee and the Politics of Health Reform* (Princeton: Princeton University Press, 1982), 123–25, 127, 131.

13. Ibid., 133–38.

14. Ibid., 141–44, 146–54.

15. Sally L. Miller, "Milwaukee: Of Ethnicity and Labor," in *Socialism and the Cities*, ed. Bruce M. Stave (Port Washington, N.Y.: Kennikat Press, 1975), 48; Leavitt, *The Healthiest City*, 154.

16. Jane Addams, *Twenty Years at Hull House* (New York: Signet, [1910] 1981), 49, 72, 81.

17. Addams, *Twenty Years,* 205.

18. Ray Stannard Baker, "Hull House and the Ward Boss," *Outlook* 58 (March 26, 1898): 769–71; *Chicago Tribune,* March 7, 1898; *Chicago Daily News,* March 11, 1898; *Picayune* [New Orleans], March 17, 1898.

19. Hull-House Residents, "An Inquiry into the Causes of the Recent Epidemic of Typhoid Fever in Chicago," *Commons* 81, no. 8 (April 1903): 3–4.

20. Ibid., 5–7.

21. Robert A. Slayton, *Back of the Yards: The Making of a Local Democracy* (Chicago: University of Chicago Press, 1986), 89–90.

22. Sylvia Hood Washington, *Packing Them In: An Archaeology of Environmental Racism in Chicago, 1865–1954* (Lanham, Md.: Lexington Books, 2004), 76, 79, 81, 85.

23. Ibid., 29; Howard Wilson, *Mary McDowell: Neighbor* (Chicago: University of Chicago Press, 1928), 146, 148–49, 151; Oscar E. Hewitt, "Talk Injunction against Garbage Dump Near Homes: Residents Say Disinfecting Will Not Avert Nuisance at North Side Site," *Chicago Daily Tribune,* October 3, 1913, 1.

24. Barbara Sicherman, ed., *Alice Hamilton: A Life in Letters* (Cambridge, Mass.: Harvard Univeristy Press, 1984), 154–55; Christopher Sellers, *Hazards of the Job: From Industrial Disease to Environmental Science* (Chapel Hill: University of North Carolina Press, 1997), 66.

25. Sicherman, ed., *Alice Hamilton,* 3–4, 154–58, 166, 181–83; Chad Montrie, *A People's History of Environmentalism in the United States* (New York: Continuum, 2011), 72–73.

26. Sicherman, ed., *Alice Hamilton,* 239; Sellers, *Hazards of the Job,* 2–3, 144, 154, 167, 22–23.

27. Lynn Page Snyder, "'The Death-Dealing Smog over Donora, Pennsylvania': Industrial Air Pollution, Public Health Policy, and the Politics of Expertise, 1948–1949," *Environmental History Review* 18, no. 1 (Spring 1994): 117–20.

28. Colin Fisher, *Urban Green: Nature, Recreation, and the Working Class in Industrial Chicago* (Chapel Hill: University of North Carolina Press, 2015), 4.

29. Ibid., 90–91.

30. Ibid., 94–96, 99.

31. Ibid., 100–103.

32. Ibid., 108–9.

33. Ibid., 115, 122–29.

34. Ibid., 130–32.

35. Ibid., 132–43.

36. Neil Maher, *Nature's New Deal: The Civilian Conservation Corps and the Roots of the American Environmental Movement* (New York: Oxford University Press, 2008), 3–4, 66.

37. Ibid., 85.

38. Joseph Speakman, *At Work in Penn's Woods: The Civilian Conservation Corps in Pennsylvania* (University Park: Pennsylvania State University Press, 2006), 103.

39. Alfred E. Cornebise, *The CCC Chronicles: Camp Newspapers of the Civilian Conservation Corps, 1933–1942* (Jefferson, N.C.: McFarland, 2004), 219–21.

40. Montrie, *A People's History of Environmentalism*, 89; Maher, *Nature's New Deal*, 10–11, 163–64.

41. Paul Sutter, *Driven Wild: How the Fight against Automobiles Launched the Modern Wilderness Movement* (Seattle: University of Washington Press, 2005), 256.

42. "CCC Realizes Dream of Col. Parker of Chain of Forest Playgrounds Here," unidentified, undated newspaper article, in "Harold Parker Forest" folder, Andover Historical Society, Andover, Mass.; *Andover Townsman,* June 1, 1934.

43. *Lawrence Eagle Tribune,* June 16, 1937.

44. Quoted in Montrie, *A People's History of Environmentalism,* 2.

45. Ibid., 101.

46. "Southern Michigan State Game Areas and Recreation Areas, 1949–1950," RG-68–6, Box 6, Folder 3, State Archives of Michigan (Lansing); *Kent League Sportsman,* October 1949, 9, in Folder 6, Box 1, "Occasional Issues of Out-of-Print Periodicals Devoted to Michigan Sports and Conservation, 1933–1965," 69–31-A, State Archives of Michigan (Lansing) [hereafter cited as SCP Collection].

47. *Genesee Sportsman,* December 1949, 4, Folder 4, Box 1, SCP Collection.

48. *Genesee Sportsman,* September 1950, 1, Folder 4, Box 1, SCP Collection; *Kent League Sportsman,* June 1949, 1, Folder 6, Box 1, SCP Collection.

49. *Macomb County Sportsman,* October 1949, 9, Folder 7, Box 1, SCP Collection; *Genesee Sportsman,* January 1949, Folder 4, Box 1, SCP Collection. See also Montrie, *A People's History of Environmentalism,* 102.

50. *Kent League Sportsman,* January 1949, 1, Folder 6, Box 1, SCP Collection; *Genesee Sportsman,* January 1949, 1, Folder 4, Box 1, SCP Collection; *Macomb County Sportsman,* September 1949, 4, Folder 7, Box 1, SCP Collection; *Saginaw Valley Sportsman,* January 1949, Folder 15, Box 1, SCP Collection.

51. Michael B. Smith, "'The Ego Ideal of the Good Camper' and the Nature of Summer Camp," *Environmental History* 11 (January 2006): 74–75, 76, 79.

52. "The FDR-CIO Labor Center Camp for Children," 1947, Folder "Camps, Children's Camp, 1950," Box 1, United Auto Workers Recreation Department Collection, Archives of Labor and Urban Affairs, Wayne State University, Detroit, Michigan [hereafter cited as UAW Recreation Collection]; Walter Reuther to Olga Madar, February 25, 1948, Folder "Camps, Children's Camp, 1948," Box 1, UAW Recreation Collection; "Children's Camp," Press Release, June 14, 1948, ibid.

53. Brochure for FDR-AFL-CIO Children's Camp (1962), Folder "Camp Folders: 1958, 1960–1962," Box 2, UAW Recreation Collection.

54. http://www2.iath.virginia.edu/sixties/HTML_docs/Resources /Primary/Manifestos/SDS_Port_Huron.html.

CHAPTER THREE. "MASSIVE MOBILIZATION
FOR A GREAT CITIZEN CRUSADE"

1. Michael B. Smith, "'Silence, Miss Carson!' Science, Gender, and the Reception of Silent Spring," *Feminist Studies* 27, no. 3 (2001): 746.

2. Rachel Carson, *Silent Spring* (Boston: Houghton Mifflin, [1962] 1987), 39.

3. Carson, *Silent Spring,* 13; Maril Hazlett, "'Woman vs. Man vs. Bugs': Gender and Popular Ecology in Early Reactions to Silent Spring," *Environmental History* 9, no. 4 (October 2004): 703–4; Gary Kroll, "The 'Silent Springs' of Rachel Carson: Mass Media and the

Origins of Modern Environmentalism," *Public Understanding of Science* 10, no. 4 (2001): 414; Michelle Mart, "Rhetoric and Response: The Cultural Impact of Rachel Carson's *Silent Spring,*" *Left History* 14, no. 2 (2009): 46.

4. Carson, *Silent Spring,* 30, 188.

5. "Pesticides: The Poisons We Eat," Folder 20, "Pesticides, Leaflets, n.d.," Box 21, UFW Administration Files; Laura Pulido, *Environmentalism and Economic Justice: Two Chicano Struggles in the Southwest* (Tucson: University of Arizona Press, [1996] 1998), 115–17.

6. Handbill to Boycotters from Delano UFWOC, November 13, 1969, Folder 18, "Pesticides, 1968–73," Box 21, United Farm Workers: Administration Files Collection, Archives of Labor and Urban Affairs, Wayne State University (Detroit Michigan) [hereafter cited as UFW Administration Files].

7. Article Draft for "The Director's Corner," Recreation Department Journal, Folder "Recreation Reports, 1945–1948," Box 2, United Auto Workers, Recreation Department Collection, Archives of Labor and Urban Affairs, Wayne State University (Detroit, Michigan).

8. Ibid.

9. Inter-Office Communication, Olga Madar to Roy Reuther, February 27, 1963, re Land and Water Conservation Fund Bill, Folder 4, "Speeches, Mar. 1963," Box 552, UAW President's Office, Walter P. Reuther Collection, Archives of Labor and Urban Affairs, Wayne State University (Detroit, Michigan) [hereafter cited as UAW President's Office Collection]. "Legislation for Recreation and Conservation," Folder 2, "Environment, 1965," Box 585, UAW President's Office Collection.

10. Walter Reuther, Opening Speech, Folder 3, "Speeches; Clear Water Conference, 6 Nov 1965," Box 555, UAW President's Office Collection.

11. "Brief History of UAW Environmental Leadership," Folder "Conservation & Recreation Depts. History, policies, and operations, 1930s–1970s," Box 11, United Auto Workers Conservation and Recreation Departments Collection, Archives of Labor and Urban Affairs, Wayne State University (Detroit Michigan) [hereafter cited as UAW

Conservation and Recreation Collection]. See also Scott Dewey, "Working for the Environment: Organized Labor and the Origins of Environmentalism in the United States, 1948–1970," *Environmental History* 3 (January 1998): 52.

12. Inter-Office Memo, Dave Czamanske to Olga Madar et al., "Summary of Activities February 1 thru April 24, 1971," Folder "Downriver Anti-Pollution League, corres. & reports, 1971–72," Box 2, UAW Conservation and Recreation Collection; *Detroit News,* April 21, 1970.

13. Winnie Fraser to Wives of UAW Officers, Board Members and Staff, August 10, 1970; Outline of Organization, October 6, 1970; and "Bus Trip Down River," all in Folder "United Active Women: UAW Wives Group," Box 8, UAW Conservation and Recreation Collection.

14. http://consblog.org/index.php/2010/04/22/a-day-for-the-earth-but-which-part/.

15. Chad Montrie, *A People's History of Environmentalism in the United States* (New York: Continuum, 2011), 107–8.

16. "Pollution Is Not a 'White Thing,'" Folder "UAW publications on the environment 1970s," Box 11, UAW Conservation and Recreation Collection.

17. David Stradling and Richard Stradling, *Where the River Burned: Carl Stokes and the Struggle to Save Cleveland* (Ithaca, N.Y.: Cornell University Press, 2015), 199, 80, 144–45.

18. Ibid., 99.

19. Ibid., 112–13.

20. Ibid., 21, 27.

21. Ibid., 161.

22. Ibid., 173–74.

23. Ibid., 197–99.

24. Quoted in David Rosner and Gerald Markowitz, "Building the World That Kills Us: The Politics of Lead, Science, and Polluted Homes, 1970 to 2000," *Journal of Urban History* 42, no. 2 (2016): 324–25.

25. On Thomas, see Robert Gioielli, *Environmental Activism and the Urban Crisis: Baltimore, St. Louis, Chicago* (Philadelphia: Temple University Press, 2014), 44, 54–55.

26. Ibid., 56, 62.

27. Ibid., 38, 50–51, 142.

28. U.S. Department of the Interior, *Study of Strip and Surface Mining in Appalachia: An Interim Report to the Appalachian Regional Commission* (Washington, D.C.: Government Printing Office, 1966), 22–24.

29. Raymond Rash to Governor Combs, September 13, 1960, and Dexter Dixon to Governor Combs, September 16, 1960, Folder 1, "Strip Mining, May 1956–Dec. 27, 1960," Box 19, Harry Caudill Papers, Special Collections, University of Kentucky (Lexington) [hereafter cited as Caudill Papers]; Chad Montrie, *To Save the Land and People: A History of Opposition to Surface Coal Mining in Appalachia* (Chapel Hill: University of North Carolina Press, 2003), 63–66.

30. *Mountain Eagle,* June 3 and 17, 1965.

31. *Hazard Herald,* November 15, 1965; Montrie, *To Save the Land and People,* 72–75, 79.

32. "Why We Came to Owensboro: A Report to Governor Breathitt, 13 July 1967," Folder 6, Box 5, Gordon Ebersole/The Congress for Appalachian Development Manuscript Collection, East Tennessee State University (Johnson City).

33. Montrie, *To Save the Land and People,* 87–88.

34. *People Speak Out on Strip Mining* (Berea, Ky.: Council of Southern Mountains, 1971), n.p.

35. Andrew W. Kahrl, "Fear of an Open Beach: Public Rights and Private Interests in 1970s Coastal Connecticut," *Journal of American History* 102 (September 2015): 439.

36. Ibid., 458–59.

37. Ibid., 437, 442.

38. Ibid., 444–46.

39. Ibid., 447.

40. Ibid., 448–49.

41. Ibid., 450–51.

42. Ibid., 451–55.

43. Ibid., 457.

44. Elizabeth Blum, *Love Canal Revisited: Race, Class, and Gender in Environmental Activism* (Lawrence: University Press of Kansas, 2008), 22.

45. Ibid., 22–24.

46. Ibid., 28.

47. Ibid., 29.

48. Ibid., 31.

49. Ibid., 57–60.

50. Ibid., 69–70, 73.

51. Ibid., 73–74.

52. Ibid., 92–93.

53. Eileen McGurty, *Transforming Environmentalism: Warren County, PCBs, and the Origins of Environmental Justice* (New Brunswick, N.J.: Rutgers University Press, 2007), 1, 41.

54. Ibid.

55. Ibid., 81, 109.

56. Ibid., 97, 113–17.

57. Ibid., 127.

58. Ibid., 128.

CONCLUSION

1. Rachel Carson, *Silent Spring* (Boston: Houghton Mifflin, [1962] 1987), 197–98.

2. Linda Lear, *Rachel Carson: Witness for Nature* (New York: Henry Holt, 1997), 429.

3. Michael B. Smith, "'Silence, Miss Carson!' Science, Gender, and the Reception of Silent Spring," *Feminist Studies* 27, no. 3 (2001): 735–38, 741.

4. Lear, *Rachel Carson,* 429–30, 433–34.

5. Smith, "'Silence, Miss Carson!'" 738.

6. Lear, *Rachel Carson,* 433–34. See also Maril Hazlett, "'Woman vs. Man vs. Bugs': Gender and Popular Ecology in Early Reactions to Silent Spring," *Environmental History* 9, no. 4 (October 2004): 706–8.

7. Lear, *Rachel Carson,* 439–40.

8. Ibid., 446–50.

9. Gary Kroll, "The 'Silent Springs' of Rachel Carson: Mass Media and the Origins of Modern Environmentalism," *Public Understanding of Science* 10, no. 4 (2001): 412–14.

10. *Charleston Gazette,* February 5, 10, 11, 1971; Chad Montrie, *To Save the Land and People: A History of Opposition to Surface Coal Mining in Appalachia* (Chapel Hill: University of North Carolina Press, 2003), 117–18.

11. Ken Hechler, press releases, April 22 and May 21, 1971, and Announcement, April 22, 1971, in Folder 6, "Strip Mining," Box 170, Ken Hechler Manuscript Collection, Special Collections, Marshall University (Huntington, W.Va.) [hereafter cited as Hechler Papers].

12. *Sierra Club Bulletin* 56 (February 1971): 7.

13. *Mining Congress Journal* 57 (September 1971): 138.

14. *United Mine Workers Journal [UMWJ]* 82 (January 1971): 6; *UMWJ* 82 (February 1971): 3; *UMWJ* 82 (March 1971): 9.

15. *Mining Congress Journal* 57 (September 1971): 138; U.S. Senate Subcommittee on Minerals, Materials, and Fuels, *Hearings before the Subcommittee on Minerals, Materials, and Fuels of the Committee of Interior and Insular Affairs Pursuant to S. Res. 45, A National Fuels and Energy Policy Study, on S. 77 . . . [and] S. 2777,* 92nd Cong., 1st sess. (1971–72), 455, 458, 473.

16. Montrie, *To Save the Land and People,* 152.

17. George W. Hopkins, "The Wheeling Convention of the Miners for Democracy: A Case Study of Union Reform Politics in Appalachia," in *Appalachia/America: The Proceedings of the 1980 Appalachian Studies Conference,* ed. Wilson Somerville (Johnson City: Appalachian Consortium Press, 1980), 11.

18. U.S. Senate Committee on Interior and Insular Affairs, *Hearings before the Committee on Interior and Insular Affairs on S. 425 . . . [and] S. 923,* 93rd Cong., 1st sess. (1973), 397–98; *UMWJ* 84 (April 1973): 14, 17, 19.

19. *UMWJ* 85 (July 1974): 5.

20. Montrie, *To Save the Land and People,* 162.

21. Senate Committee on Interior and Insular Affairs, *Hearings . . . on S. 425,* 911–15; U.S. House of Representatives, Subcommittee on the Environment and Subcommittee on Mines and Mining, *Hearings before the Subcommittee on the Environment and Subcommittee on Mines and Mining of the Committee on Interior and Insular Affairs on H.R. 3 and Related Bills, Relating to Strip Mining,* 92d Cong., 1st sess. (1975), 1645–46; Ned Helmes to Ken Hechler, March 30[, 1973], Folder 7, "Strip Mining," Box 170, Hechler Papers; Ken Hechler to Friends of the Coalition against Strip Mining, January 18, 1975, Folder 8, "Strip Mining," Box 170, Hechler Papers; Montrie, *To Save the Land and People,* 162–63.

22. *World-News,* April 9 and 14, 1975.

23. U.S. House of Representatives, Subcommittee on Energy and the Environment and Subcommittee on Mines and Mining, *Hearings before the Subcommittee on Energy and Environment and the Subcommittee on Mines and Mining of the Committee on Interior and Insular Affairs on the President's Veto of H.R. 25*, 94th Cong., 1st sess. (1975), 13–17; "Declaration of Policy," *Mining Congress Journal* 61 (November 1975): 89; United Mine Workers of America, *Proceedings of the 47th Constitutional Convention* (Cincinnati, Ohio: United Mine Workers of America, 1976), 273–76.

24. *Charleston Gazette,* June 6, 1999.

25. *Charleston Gazette-Mail,* June 2, 2014. See also Montrie, *A People's History of Environmentalism,* 137, 172.

26. Les Leopold, *The Man Who Hated Work and Loved Labor: The Life and Times of Tony Mazzochi* (White River Junction, Vt.: Chelsea Green, 2007), 230.

27. Ibid., 235, 245–48.

28. Ibid., 246, 253 (quote), 272.

29. Ibid., 247.

30. Ibid., 281; Robert Gordon, "Environmental Blues: Working-Class Environmentalism and the Labor-Environmental Alliance" (Ph.D. diss., Wayne State University, 2004), 55; Chad Montrie, *A People's History of Environmentalism,* 112.

31. Robert Gordon, "'Shell No!': OCAW and the Labor-Environmental Alliance," *Environmental History* 3 (October 1998): 468–70, 472–73.

32. Ibid., 474–75.

33. Timothy Minchin, *Forging a Common Bond: Labor Activism during the BASF Lockout* (Gainesville: University Press of Florida, 2003), 59–60.

34. Ibid., 1–3; Gordon, "Environmental Blues," 336.

35. Minchin, *Forging a Common Bond,* 2, 154–55 (quotes), 158. See also Jim Schwab, *Deeper Shades of Green: The Rise of Blue-Collar and Minority Environmentalism in America* (San Francisco: Sierra Club Books, 1994).

36. Baird Straughn and Tom Pollak, *The Broader Movement: Nonprofit Environmental and Conservation Organizations, 1989–2005* (Washington, D.C.: Urban Institute, National Center for Charitable Statistics, 2008), 7, 25; Mark Dowie, *Losing Ground: American Environmentalism at the Close of the Twentieth Century* (Cambridge, Mass.: MIT Press, 1995), 40–41.

FURTHER READING

Blum, Elizabeth. *Love Canal Revisited: Race, Class, and Gender in Environmental Activism.* Lawrence: University Press of Kansas, 2008.

Cumbler, John. *Reasonable Use: The People, Environment, and the State, New England 1790–1930.* New York: Oxford University Press, 2001.

Fisher, Colin. *Urban Green: Nature, Recreation, and the Working Class in Industrial Chicago.* Chapel Hill: University of North Carolina Press, 2015.

Gioielli, Robert. *Environmental Activism and the Urban Crisis: Baltimore, St. Louis, Chicago.* Philadelphia: Temple University Press, 2014.

Gordon, Robert. "Environmenal Blues: Working-Class Environmentalism and the Labor-Environmental Alliance." PhD diss., Wayne State University, 2004.

———. "Poisons in the Fields: The United Farm Workers, Pesticides, and Environmental Politics." *Pacific Historical Review* 68 (February 1999): 51–77.

———. "'Shell No!': OCAW and the Labor-Environmental Alliance." *Environmental History* 3 (October 1998): 460–87.

Hurley, Andrew. *Environmental Inequalities: Class, Race, and Industrial Pollution in Gary, Indiana, 1945–1980.* Chapel Hill: University of North Carolina Press, 1995.

Jacoby, Karl. *Crimes against Nature: Squatters, Poachers, Thieves, and the Hidden History of American Conservation.* Berkeley: University of California Press, 2001.

Kahrl, Andrew W. "Fear of an Open Beach: Public Rights and Private Interests in 1970s Coastal Connecticut." *Journal of American History* 102 (September 2015): 433–62.

Leopold, Les. *The Man Who Hated Work and Loved Labor.* White River Junction, Vt.: Chelsea Green, 2007.

Lipin, Lawrence. *Workers and the Wild: Conservation, Consumerism, and Labor in Oregon, 1910–1930.* Urbana: University of Illinois Press, 2007.

Maher, Neil. *Nature's New Deal: The Civilian Conservation Corps and the Roots of the American Environmental Movement.* New York: Oxford University Press, 2008.

McGurty, Eileen. *Transforming Environmentalism: Warren County , PCBs, and the Origins of the Environmental Justice Movement.* New Brunswick, N.J.: Rutgers University Press, 2009.

Montrie, Chad. *To Save the Land and People: A History of Opposition to Surface Coal Mining in Appalachia.* Chapel Hill: University of North Carolina Press, 2003.

——. *Making a Living: Work and Environment in the United States.* Chapel Hill: University of North Carolina Press, 2008.

——. *A People's History of Environmentalism in the United States.* New York: Continuum, 2011.

Pulido, Laura. *Environmentalism and Economic Justice: Two Chicano Struggles in the Southwest.* Tucson: University of Arizona Press, [1996] 1998.

Sellers, Christopher. *Hazards of the Job: From Industrial Disease to Environmental Science.* Chapel Hill: University of North Carolina Press, 1997.

Spence, Mark David. *Dispossessing the Wilderness: Indian Removal and the Making of the National Parks.* New York: Oxford University Press, 1999.

Stradling, David, and Richard Stradling. *Where the River Burned: Carl Stokes and the Struggle to Save Cleveland.* Ithaca, N.Y.: Cornell University Press, 2015.

Warren, Louis. *The Hunter's Game: Poachers and Conservationists in Twentieth-Century America.* New Haven, Conn.: Yale University Press, 1997.

INDEX